MILESTONES
IN
AMERICAN HISTORY

THE DONNER PARTY

MILESTONES
IN
AMERICAN HISTORY

THE ACQUISITION OF FLORIDA

THE ALAMO

ALEXANDER GRAHAM BELL
AND THE TELEPHONE

THE ATTACK ON PEARL HARBOR

THE CALIFORNIA GOLD RUSH

THE CIVIL RIGHTS ACT OF 1964

THE DONNER PARTY

THE ELECTRIC LIGHT

THE EMANCIPATION PROCLAMATION

THE ERIE CANAL

THE LOUISIANA PURCHASE

MANIFEST DESTINY

THE MONROE DOCTRINE

THE OREGON TRAIL

THE OUTBREAK OF THE CIVIL WAR

THE PONY EXPRESS

THE PROHIBITION ERA

THE ROBBER BARONS AND THE
SHERMAN ANTITRUST ACT

THE SINKING OF THE USS *MAINE*

SPUTNIK/EXPLORER I

THE STOCK MARKET CRASH OF 1929

THE TRANSCONTINENTAL RAILROAD

THE TREATY OF PARIS

THE WRIGHT BROTHERS

MILESTONES
IN
AMERICAN HISTORY
★ ★ ☆ ★ ★ ☆ ★ ★ ★ ★ ★ ☆ ★ ★ ☆ ★ ★

THE
DONNER PARTY

A DOOMED JOURNEY

TIM MCNEESE

CHELSEA HOUSE
PUBLISHERS
An imprint of Infobase Publishing

The Donner Party

Copyright © 2009 by Infobase Publishing

Chelsea House
An imprint of Infobase Publishing
132 West 31st Street
New York NY 10001

Library of Congress Cataloging-in-Publication Data
McNeese, Tim.
  The Donner Party : a doomed journey / Tim McNeese.
     p. cm. — (Milestones in American history)
  Includes bibliographical references and index.
  ISBN 978-1-60413-025-6 (hardcover)
  1. Donner Party—Juvenile literature. 2. Pioneers—California—History—19th century—Juvenile literature. 3. Pioneers—West (U.S.)—History—19th century—Juvenile literature. 4. Pioneers—California—Biography—Juvenile literature. 5. Overland journeys to the Pacific—Juvenile literature. 6. Frontier and pioneer life—West (U.S.)—Juvenile literature. 7. Sierra Nevada (Calif. and Nev.)—History—19th century—Juvenile literature. I. Title. II. Series.

  F868.N5M35 2009
  979.4'3703—dc22   2008029652

Series design by Erik Lindstrom
Cover design by Ben Peterson

Printed in the United States of America

Bang FOF 10 9 8 7 6 5 4 3 2 1

This book is printed on acid-free paper.

CONTENTS

1   The Stevens Party   1

2   A Vision Looking West   10

3   Wagons to California   20

4   The First "Donner Party"   32

5   Progress on the Trail   45

6   A Badly Advised Road   56

7   Tragedy at Every Turn   68

8   The Taboo   79

9   "Do You Come from Heaven?"   93

10   Nightmare's End   106

11   Lives of the Survivors   120

Chronology and Timeline   130

Notes   135

Bibliography   138

Further Reading   140

Index   142

The Stevens Party

They were traveling westward by the thousands, in long, snaky trains of dozens of covered wagons. Each wagon carried scores of emigrant pioneers from the East; all eager to find what opportunities lay ahead. They followed in the tracks of those who had blazed the Oregon Trail—first American Indians, then mountain men, then missionaries. The trail to Oregon, which split off in a great geographic fork in the road to deliver some hearty souls to California, was a western road representing challenge and danger. It was not a road for the timid. By the late 1830s and early 1840s, however, the Oregon Trail, the route the American Indians called "the Great Medicine Road," was becoming a super-highway of migration.

Pioneers, also called settlers, have played an important role in American history because they formed the societal structure for those who followed. Pioneer families traveled to unexplored territory in search of a new life and had to deal with many hardships, including poor equipment, illness, and attacks by American Indians.

WAGONS TO CALIFORNIA

It was not until 1843 to 1844 that an emigrant wagon train managed to cross the Sierra Nevada Mountains to California without having to abandon its wagons. The party that made it included 26 men, 8 women, and 17 children. Many in the party of ox-drawn wagons were Irish, and about a half-dozen of these families were intermarried. Another wagon belonged to a former mountain man named Isaac Hitchcock who traveled with his widowed daughter and her children. Another family wagon included a Dr. John Townshend and his wife, as well as the wife's 17-year-old brother, Moses Schallenberger, who would keep a journal of the expedition.

Three additional wagons filled out the train, owned by two other families and a single man, Elisha Stevens. A "slight, wiry man of about 40,"[1] Stevens was a blacksmith by trade. Although he had not traveled the Oregon Trail previously, he had lived in the northwestern frontier while working in the fur trade. He shared the leadership of the wagon party with a long-time mountain man and veteran of the western road, Caleb Greenwood, who was accompanied by two mixed blood sons. The sons served as additional guides and American Indian interpreters. Lastly, several young, unmarried men moved along the trail with pack animals.

On May 18, 1843, the Stevens Party set out on the Oregon Trail from their base along the west bank of the Missouri River, opposite Council Bluffs, in modern-day Iowa. The first leg of their trip on the Oregon Trail went without serious incident. Stevens provided disciplined leadership and kept dissension among the party's members to a minimum. When the train arrived west of South Pass in the Rocky Mountains, Greenwood suggested taking a dicey shortcut called Hastings Cutoff that would shave 85 miles off their route.

The party managed to reach Fort Hall, in modern-day Idaho, northwest of Soda Springs along the Snake River. The date was August 10, and they still had hundreds of miles before they reached California. After resting several days, the wagon train hit the trail again, moving along the Snake River. Two days out from Fort Hall, the party turned south to follow the Raft River Valley upstream. Largely, the Stevens train followed the trail to the Humboldt Sink in modern-day Nevada, where the alkali water-way petered out. The party's progress floundered for a week, with everyone uncertain as to where to proceed next.

Then, a band of Paiute appeared at Humboldt Sink. Greenwood sat down with the party's chief, whose name sounded to the old mountain man like "Truckee." (The word actually was not the chief's name at all, but rather a Paiute word that could be translated as "all right," or "very well," or even "okay.") Through sign language, the chief explained that he knew the location of Sutter's Fort, the wagon party's goal in California, and that he knew the best route to get the pioneers to it. John Augustus Sutter, a Swiss immigrant, had entered Mexican California less than a decade earlier. Gaining a significant land grant from the Mexican government, he had established a large ranch, which became a destination for settlers on the California Trail. Sitting down on the ground, the Paiute leader drew a map in the dirt, indicating the existence of a river to the west, just two days away. That river flowed eastward, out of a tall canyon. Beyond the canyon lay another river that flowed to Sutter's Fort. At last, the Stevens Party had its bearings.

NEW DIRECTIONS ON THE TRAIL

They began their western trek on the morning of October 8, covering more or less the same territory spanned by Highway 40 today. Stevens kept his party moving long after midnight. By 2 P.M. the following day, the emigrants reached the river forecast by the Paiute chief. There, the party was about 35 miles from modern-day Reno, Nevada. After 32 hours of nonstop travel on the trail, the wagon train's livestock was near exhaustion. Then the party began their crossing of the Forty-Mile Desert, a forbidding stretch of the trail. The desert required two grueling days to cross. It proved so difficult that Schallenberger, in his journal, estimated the distance as twice what it actually was. Once across the desert, Stevens let the tired animals rest, even though they were about to encounter winter weather.

Significant problems loomed ahead for the Stevens Party. They were heading into the Sierra Nevada. Probably on October 12, they moved west along the river they would name for the Paiute chief, Truckee. Progress proved slow, with the party sometimes covering no more than two or three miles in a day. There were constant inclines, and the wagons had to be unloaded and even kept upright using special ropes. Further slowing down the party were the constant river crossings, as many as three or four times a day, back and forth across the same mountain stream. Snows fell on the party, piling up so deep that the oxen and horses could not find grass to eat. A pair of oxen starved to death. The oxen's hooves were softening as well, causing several to become lame. The humans were having a difficult time as well, with the men almost constantly having to wade through icy mountain streams during river crossings.

The trail was turning against the Stevens Party, and yet, they pressed on, reaching modern-day Truckee, California, on November 14. They had only covered 70 miles in 32 days of grueling, backbreaking labor. Snow continued to fall. In a panic, six members of the party—four men considered to be the party's best hunters, and two women—went ahead of the main party in hopes of finding help at Sutter's ranch. The six members of the advance party climbed the hills along the Truckee River until they reached the western shores of a mountain lake. It was there that they discovered a pass through the snow-capped mountains, which led them to a westward-flowing river, probably the Middle Fork of the American River. They had no food other than the game they killed, and river crossings kept them cold and wet. But on December 10, they reached Sutter's Fort.

In the meantime, the emigrant wagon train followed the western branch of the Truckee River for two or three miles until it reached what would come to be known as Donner Lake. At the lake, they discussed what to do next. They chose to abandon six wagons and continue on with the remaining five. Three young men were left behind to guard the abandoned wagons; two were named Joseph Foster and Allen Montgomery, and the third was Moses Schallenberger, the journal keeper and Dr. Townshend's brother-in-law. Of major concern for Townshend was the cargo of his own wagon: a large collection of broadcloth, silks, and other light fabrics in which he had invested his life's savings. His plan had been to sell them at high prices in California. If they were left behind, American Indians might steal them, leaving him destitute.

Pictured is Donner Lake, located in the town of Truckee, California. Major emigrant trails run near the lake, and it was a major avenue for pioneers who were heading west through the Sierra Nevada.

As the scaled-down wagon party pressed on, the emigrants began to climb out of the canyon that surrounded them. In some places the snow was several feet deep and the "mountain was so steep that an empty wagon could hardly be taken up."[2] At one point, "oxen had to be led up through a narrow defile, then a wagon dragged to the top with half a dozen yokes straining at chains while men hoisted from below."[3] The party took five days to climb to the summit of the pass, to an altitude of 7,189 feet. (It would become known as Donner Pass.)

Although the strain of traversing the pass was behind them, there were other challenges still ahead. About 20 miles beyond Donner Pass, a blinding snowstorm hit. When the storm began to die down, 17 of the party's young men set out for the sanctuary of Sutter's Fort, leaving behind the two oldest men, along with the women and children. The men reached the Swiss captain's ranch on December 13, in time to meet a rescue party heading east toward the wagon train. Soon, those left back at the wagons were discovered and brought to Sutter's Fort.

As for the three men left to protect the abandoned wagons, two of them arrived in Sacramento Valley a few weeks later. They told a story of bitter winter weather and of their low food supplies, which led them to leave their wagons behind or face certain death. When asked about the third member of their group, Moses Schallenberger, they explained how he had become too weak to travel, and how they had abandoned him to die. Surprisingly, in February 1844, Schallenberger limped into the valley in the company of rescuers, alive, even if in poor shape.

SCHALLENBERGER'S STARVATION STORY

The story of what happened to those three men left to fend for themselves with few supplies in the midst of intimidating winter snows was an adventure in itself. Of the three young men, Schallenberger's story would become the most compelling. He had agreed to stay behind to guard his brother-in-law's wagon because he "did not suppose that the snow would at any time be more than two feet deep, or that it would be on the ground continually."[4] Schallenberger was an excellent hunter, and so the departing party left little food behind, believing that he would not need it. Stevens himself decided to leave behind two scrawny milk cows that were unable to continue the journey. They could provide the trio of young men with milk and, in a pinch, could be slaughtered for meat.

Almost as soon as the main party continued on its way toward Donner Pass, the three men soon found themselves in the midst of a violent snowstorm. The snows piled up to a depth of four feet, cutting off any grasses the cows might need for food. Hunting provided little meat, and after a few days the three men had finished what food had been left for them. They then butchered the two cows, which, because they were so thin, provided little meat.

As the snows piled up, so did the days the men were forced to endure these difficulties. By mid-December, they had little food left. The threat of starvation loomed before them, and the three young men were forced to make a serious decision. If they remained with the abandoned wagons, they might die; but taking off on the trail would be risky as well. None of them had snowshoes. Undaunted, Schallenberger's two companions, Foster and Montgomery, fashioned three pairs of makeshift snowshoes out of ox-bows and rawhide. As they worked, Schallenberger cut the last of their remaining meat supply into strips to dry into jerky. They then set out, bound for Sutter's Fort, just as their trail companions had earlier.

Things did not go well. Foster and Montgomery had made the snowshoes incorrectly, binding them to the men's feet at both heel and toe, instead of just at the toe. Since they were fastened at the heel, too, the men had to raise their feet straight up, lifting snow as they went as if they had shovels strapped to their feet. As they awkwardly climbed up Donner Pass, Schallenberger tired quickly and began to suffer from leg cramps. The other two men were able to continue, but Schallenberger could not. Nearly crippled, he opted to turn around and head back to the wagons. Foster and Montgomery gave him most of the remaining meat, with the hopes that a rescue party would find him before he starved to death.

Schallenberger, even with his leg problems, did not sit back and wait to either die or be rescued. He remembered some of the wagons still held animal traps, and he had seen fox and coyote tracks in the snow. For weeks, he managed to survive on the foxes he caught, roasting them on an open fire. As for coyote, he could not stomach the taste of their meat. Living by his skills and his wits, Schallenberger managed to stay alive until he was rescued by Dr. Townshend's hired hands on February 26, 1844.

The Stevens Party had achieved its goal of reaching California along the Oregon and California trails, becoming the first emigrant party to succeed in taking its wagons all the way to the Sacramento Valley. Perhaps even more amazing, not a single member of the party had been lost. Once they entered the California Trail, they had faced almost constant challenge and difficulty, but they had found their way along rivers, alkali flats, canyons, and even mountains. Ultimately, the Stevens Party succeeded in its journey to California because its members cooperated, made rational and reasonable decisions, and made timely progress along the trail. Three years later, the now-infamous Donner Party followed much of the same route and experienced many of the same physical difficulties. The fate of the Donner Party, however, was as different from that of the Stevens Party as night is from day.

A Vision
Looking West

Today, after a century and a half of history, the wagon ruts remain. Here and there, in western Nebraska, in Wyoming, and even west of the Continental Divide, rock outcroppings are still scarred from the thousands of wagons that passed over them, as caravans of emigrants moved along the Oregon Trail bound for the Oregon Country (the modern-day states of Oregon, Washington, and Idaho) or California. Parts of the old trail are still visible to those who explore along Nebraska's Platte River Valley, the Wyoming tablelands, or the alkali flats of Nevada. From various jumping-off places in western Missouri—Independence, Westport (today's Kansas City), St. Joseph, Weston—the wagons carried families along the 2,000-mile western trail, crossing the Great Plains, the foothills of the Rockies, and the high country gap in the mountains known as South Pass, to a fork in the road. At that split, some took the

The wheels of the thousands of wagons that traveled the trails eventually cut ruts, or sunken tracks, more than two feet deep through a rock ridge on the trail. The sides and bottoms of the wagons also cut grooves, or troughs, six feet wide and four feet deep through the rock as the wagons dragged over it. Today, these ruts are embedded in sandstone formations on the High Plains prairie near Guernsey, Wyoming.

road to the left—the California Trail—while others bore to the right to remain on the Oregon Trail to the Pacific Northwest.

THE LURE OF OREGON

In all, between the 1840s and 1860s, a third of a million people walked or rode these routes. Some were farmers from back East, ready to plow the fertile lands of the Willamette River Valley. Others were gold seekers headed to California, all in a rush, excited by the stories of uncovered riches along the American and Sacramento rivers. Others went to the West to plant missionary settlements, fur trading posts, and trail stores to supply other emigrants with goods who came after them on the same trails.

THE BIDWELL-BARTLESON PARTY

The first true wagon trains that traveled the Oregon Trail did not hit the great western road until the early 1840s. These trains carried family units that included fathers, mothers, and children, even infants. When these early pioneers set out westward, they were so naive that it is a wonder they even made the trip at all.

The first overland party that took to the trail left Missouri bound for California in 1841. The party was organized by a traveling schoolteacher named John Bidwell. He was "handsome, intelligent, and imbued with a pioneer spirit."[1] Despite any specific experience traveling across the Far West, Bidwell succeeded in convincing 500 people to join his would-be wagon train, the Western Emigration Society. As Bidwell himself conceded: "Our ignorance of the route was complete. We knew that California lay west, and that was the extent of our knowledge."[2]

That spring, hundreds of eager adventure seekers who had signed on with Bidwell over the previous year were scheduled to meet at Sapling Grove, located in the modern-day state of Kansas. This jumping-off place had served for 20 years as part of the Santa Fe Trail and was located 20 miles west of

Independence, Missouri. Bidwell had instructed his people to reach Sapling Grove by May 19, but when he arrived that day, only one wagon of emigrants was ready to hit the road. It seems that many had been influenced to abandon the caravan after reading stories in U.S. newspapers that winter "of an American being tossed into a California jail for simply suggesting the United States might someday take possession of that Mexican-held territory."[3] Others were scared off by a letter that returning emigrant Thomas Farnham wrote. Farnham had reached Oregon, but left the western country greatly discouraged. The letter showed up that spring in various newspapers in the Midwest. Bad news gave rise to doubts, and the Bidwell Party suffered even more dropouts.

Undeterred, Bidwell waited a few more days until 69 emigrants had gathered with their wagons, all ready to make their way to the West. When they left Sapling Grove, the members of the party were uncertain whether they wanted to follow the trail to Oregon or California. Ironically, although Bidwell had organized the party, another member of the Western Emigration Society, John Bartleson, was selected as the actual leader. It was an appointment that Bartleson won only after he threatened to leave the group, along with eight of his burly friends, if he was not chosen. With no clear direction and starting out under circumstances that were less than ideal, the Bidwell-Bartleson Party set out. As Bidwell noted, though, "No one knew where to go, not even the captain."[4]

Once on the trail, they were fortunate to catch up with a veteran of the western road, a former mountain man named Thomas Fitzpatrick. He was a "slender and intelligent Irishman"[5] dubbed "Broken Hand" by the Cheyenne after a misfired rifle blew off three of his fingers. Fitzpatrick, an old associate of famed American fur man Jim Bridger, was on the trail leading a trio of Jesuit missionaries. The trio, which included Father Pierre Jean De Smet, was headed to the Oregon Country to minister to the western American Indians. Although

Wagon trains traveled together in caravans. These large groups provided protection and mutual assistance for settlers. The captain, also called the wagon master, led the group and made any decisions that affected the whole caravan. At night the wagons formed a circle for protection against American Indians and other marauders, and to keep their animals from running away.

the Bidwell-Bartleson Party had not yet decided on its final destination—California or Oregon—Fitzpatrick agreed to lead them for the first 1,200 miles of the trail. Then, beyond South Pass, they would have to make their decision.

As the party continued, few things went well. They did manage to make good time to the first major stop on the trail, Wyoming's Fort Laramie. From there, they moved on another 500 miles to Soda Springs in modern-day Idaho. The party was nearly stampeded by bison one night, only managing to save themselves by lighting campfires to steer away the animals. Then they were pelted with hail during a violent rainstorm that delivered a giant tornado within a quarter-mile of the wagons. In another incident, Bidwell's friend Nicholas Dawson strayed too far from the wagon train and found himself at the mercy of a band of Cheyenne, who stole his mule and guns and forced him to strip off his clothes. He was called "Cheyenne Dawson" by the rest of the party after that.

The emigrants fell into squabbles until the party split off into two groups. When they reached the Bear River, Fitzpatrick, Father De Smet, and his fellow Jesuits took the north trail toward Oregon. Most of the Bidwell-Bartleson Party chose to go along with them, having come to depend on Fitzpatrick's leadership. Bidwell and a party of nine wagons with 34 emigrants, including a woman and her child, took the left fork toward California.

They had lost their guide, since Fitzpatrick continued on to Oregon, and they had only the broadest sense of how to reach their goal. Everyone in the party "only knew that California lay to the west."[6] The land before them was treacherous and unrelenting. The directions Fitzpatrick gave them before his departure were to keep to the Bear River until they arrived at the Valley of the Great Salt Lake (in modern-day Utah, then Mexican territory). Once they skirted around the lake's northern shore, they were to continue west to the Humboldt River, which would lead them to California.

The advance of the Bidwell Party was nothing short of a struggle. Once they rounded the Great Salt Lake, they crossed into the desolate, dry lands of northern Nevada. Their food began to run out, and wild game became scarce. Reaching the Humboldt, they abandoned their wagons, considering them an impediment to their progress. Traveling now on foot, the party butchered their oxen for food. Later they met with local

(continues on page 18)

JOHN AUGUSTUS SUTTER
(1803-1880)

A Swiss Fugitive in California

The decade of the 1840s would deliver the first wagon trains of emigrants from the East to California by way of the California Trail. When the Bidwell Party reached California, it arrived in one of the Mexican territory's lush valleys, the San Joaquin. Bidwell would move to another great California valley, the Sacramento, where he came under the employ of a Swiss immigrant named John Sutter. When gold was discovered on Sutter's ranch in 1848, Sutter became one of the most famous Californians. He also, it appears, was a man with a few skeletons in his closet.

When Sutter arrived in San Francisco Bay onboard a sailing ship in 1839, he found California a place in turmoil. California had been a northern province of the Spanish empire for hundreds of years and a Mexican province for less than 20 following the successful overthrow of the Spanish colonial government by the Mexican people in 1821. But revolution in California did not end then. California was so far north of the capital of Mexico City that "the bonds between the two were weak."[*] In regional revolutions, the Spanish-speaking residents of the region, the *Californios*, overthrew more than one provincial governor thrust on them by Mexico City. There was even occasional talk of fighting for independence from the Mexican government. Only the existence of regional rivalries and personal disputes kept those unhappy with Mexico City from banding together toward this common goal.

Despite such political turmoil, the California of the 1830s and 1840s began to draw a significant number of foreign immigrants, mostly from the United States. Since California was such an immense piece of property and its non–American Indian population was so small, these new arrivals were given generous land grants to establish ranches and farming fields.

Enter John Sutter, who received nearly 50,000 acres of prime California land from Mexican governor Pio Pico, with whom Sutter ingratiated himself. His land was situated in the fertile Sacramento Valley, northeast of present-day San Francisco, in two sections: one along the Feather River and the second at the confluence of the Sacramento and American rivers.

Sutter's future seemed certain, while his past was a mystery to many. When Sutter left his native Switzerland, he was little more than a fugitive from justice. He had left a failing dry goods and drapery business that was on the verge of bankruptcy. He also escaped a mountain of unpaid bills, bad debts, and "a domineering wife and five children."** When Sutter boarded a ship to sail to the United States, various European officials were issuing out warrants for his arrest.

Nevertheless, Sutter was able to recreate himself while in California. From a hilltop overlooking the American River, where gold was discovered nearly a decade later, Sutter had a formidable adobe fortress constructed and manned by local American Indian laborers. He built an extensive personal enclave over which he presided, complete with his own gristmill, tannery, and workshops. His workers harvested grains from his fields and fruit from his orchards, and tended large herds of cattle and sheep. Sutter, perhaps missing his homeland, named his colony *Nueva Helvetia*, or "New Switzerland."

Sutter's Fort became a popular destination for immigrants who arrived along the California Trail. Sutter was hospitable and always generous, especially to immigrants from the United States. Eventually, Sutter would raise the U.S. flag over his personal fortress and pledge his allegiance to the United States even while

(continues)

(continued)

California remained, at least for the moment, Mexican territory. After Sutter hired Bidwell to work as his clerk, one of Bidwell's duties was to transfer the contents of an abandoned Russian trading post in Northern California. Among the items Bidwell delivered to Sutter's Fort were several French cannons, which Sutter set up at his fort in case he ever had trouble with the Mexican government.

* *David Lavender*, The American Heritage History of The Great West. *New York: American Heritage Publishing, 1965, 217.*
** *Tom Bodett*, America's Historic Trails. *San Francisco: KQED Books, 1997, 177.*

(continued from page 15)

American Indians, poor residents of the desert, and bartered for food. (At one point, American Indians offered the weary emigrants "a gummy concoction that turned out to be mashed insects."[7])

They pressed on, staying close to the Humboldt, which steered to the southwest, until they reached the Sierra Nevada at Sonora Pass. This placed them farther south than most future wagon companies would travel. Down to eating little but boiled acorns and slaughtered mules and horses, they finally reached the Stanislaus River and then limped into California's San Joaquin Valley, which must have seemed like nothing short of paradise. They had traveled 2,000 miles over seven months, but they had made the trip successfully and against incredible odds. In the valley, they were relieved to meet a local rancher named

John Marsh, a Harvard graduate and nearly self-taught medical doctor. (Marsh's stories about the idyllic life in California had run in newspapers back East. Several in the Bidwell Party had read such accounts.)

These emigrants were among the first to travel the California Trail. Technically, though, they were not the first wagon party to reach California, since they had abandoned their wagons back along the Humboldt. Still, their success was notable. As one historian pointed out, summing up the importance of the Bidwell Party's success, "Considering that they had no knowledge of the geography of the West, no one to guide them, and no frontier experience, their achievement is one of the most amazing in American history."[8]

Members of the party soon went their separate ways. John Bidwell moved on to the Sacramento Valley, where he took up work as chief clerk for California rancher and Swiss immigrant John Sutter. California proved to be a gold mine for Bidwell. It was on Sutter's ranch that gold was first discovered seven years later, which led to a deluge of hungry gold seekers, most of whom followed the California Trail. On site at the beginning of the gold rush, Bidwell was fortunate enough to strike it rich in the gold diggings, making enough money to purchase a 26,000-acre ranch. He was even able to establish his own town, the settlement of Chico. A lifelong success, he ran for U.S. president in 1892 on the Prohibition Party's ticket. He died in 1900, nearly 60 years after he had successfully conquered the California Trail.

Wagons
to California

Despite the success of the Bidwell Party in reaching California, the vast majority of those who went to the West over the next two or three years did not go to California, but to the Oregon Country. California was a country, after all, still owned by Mexico. The United States at least had a partial claim to Oregon, along with the British, whose fur traders had reached the region long before there was even a United States. If the United States were to stake a claim to any lands west of the Rocky Mountains in the 1840s, most believed it would have to be in Oregon.

The region certainly had its promoters, including a minister from the East, Jason Lee, and Hall Jackson Kelley, who had once owned a textile mill in New England. Kelley had read an edition of *The Journals of Lewis and Clark*, which sparked his imagination and turned him into a human drumbeat for immigration to Oregon. Hundreds, even thousands, began turning their eyes toward Oregon. In 1844, the Boston newspaper the *Daily Evening Transcript* reported, "Hundreds are already prepared to start [for Oregon] in the spring. . . . The Oregon Fever has broken out, and is now raging like any other contagion."[1]

A CHANGE IN THE TRAIL

Still, not everyone took the Oregon Trail into the Pacific Northwest. Others followed the Bidwell Party between 1841 and 1843. As the California Trail gained greater use, the trail was altered and improved. The southbound cutoff was straightened out and some of its more treacherous aspects eliminated. Even still, it remained a formidable road.

Holding back its wholesale use was the failure of anyone to successfully take wagons along the trail all the way to California. Even today, the question of who reached California first by wagon along the California Trail is controversial. During the summer of 1843, Joe Walker led a small train of wagons, known as the Chiles Party, into a region that is today part of California, although at the time, it was not. The Chiles train consisted of three mule-driven wagons, as well as several pack and saddle horses. The party left Fort Hall, taking the Snake River to the Humboldt, and then continued on the same route Walker had taken out of California back in 1834. It was in the Owens Valley (today part of eastern California) that the Walker-led party gave up its wagons, choosing to cross the Sierra Nevada with only the pack animals.

Despite its severe difficulties, the Stevens Party would succeed in taking wagons the entire length of the California Trail by 1844. Word of the success of the Stevens Party spread back East, encouraging more people to take the trail to California. As interest in California grew, Mexican officials there became increasingly alarmed. The Mexican population in California was small, and the more people who left the United States for its fertile valleys—such as the Sonora or the Sacramento—the

This drawing depicts Joe Walker (1798–1876), mountaineer and scout. He was called one of the bravest and skilled of the mountain men. Walker and the largest beaver hunting party at that time were hired to explore the Great Salt Lake and to find an overland route to California. The pass he discovered at the base of the Sierra Nevada is now called Walker Pass.

more "they cast a shadow over Mexico's ability to maintain its control of that vast territory."[2] A worried Mexican official, California governor Pio Pico, wrote a letter to his superiors in Mexico City:

> We find ourselves threatened by hordes of Yankee migrants, who have already begun to flock into our country, and whose progress we cannot arrest. Already have the wagons of that perfidious people scaled the almost inaccessible summits of the Sierra Nevada, crossed the entire continent and penetrated the fruitful valley of the Sacramento. What that astonishing people will next undertake, I cannot say.[3]

A MAN OF CONFIDENCE

As more and more emigrants made their way along the California Trail, the route was almost constantly tweaked, as pioneers discovered a shorter way to a river or a way of bypassing a particularly rugged stretch of the trail. Trail guides provided emigrants with the latest routes and tips for a successful migration. Lansford W. Hastings, a young lawyer from Ohio, wrote one such emigrant guide in 1845. Hastings's *The Emigrants' Guide to Oregon and California* became commonly used, and in fact, would influence the Donner Party to take a questionable cutoff on the California Trail. It was a tip that promised a short trail ride, but it may have been a poor suggestion in reality.

In 1842, Hastings had been a part of the second organized wagon emigration company bound for Oregon. (The first had been the Bidwell-Bartleson Party of the previous year.) That 1842 party's leader was Dr. Elijah White, a former missionary who had come out to Oregon during the 1830s to minister to the western American Indians. The party left Independence on May 16 and made good progress across Kansas and Nebraska, reaching Fort Laramie (in present-day Wyoming) on July 3.

With the hardest portion of the trail still ahead, White hired Thomas Fitzpatrick, a veteran Westerner and mountain man, as his party's guide. Fitzpatrick had led the Bidwell Party the previous year.

A few days later, the train passed Independence Rock, a massive outcropping, where Hastings and another member of the emigrant train left the trail to carve their names on the rock, as many trail emigrants did. Their venture did not go well. While cutting their signatures in stone, the two men were suddenly surrounded and taken captive by several hundred Lakota warriors. Although Hastings and his friend were released after only a few hours, his adventures in the West were just beginning.

The following year, Hastings sailed from Oregon to California, where he sought opportunities for himself. He left California, taking a ship to Mexico and then around the tip of South America back East. In 1845, he was back on the Oregon Trail and turned southwest to take the California Trail back into northern California. He and his party did not reach the Sierra Nevada until December and were barely able to crest the mountains before reaching Sutter's Fort on Christmas Day, ahead of a massive snowstorm.

Back in California, it once again became clear to Hastings that the Mexican government's hold on California was tenuous, and he soon began scheming a way to increase the number of U.S. immigrants in the rich northern Mexican province. If immigrants from the east began pouring into California as they were beginning to do in Oregon, the Mexican government might be overthrown and the region would become U.S. territory. After all, that same series of events had taken place in Texas during the 1830s. Hastings was soon at work on his emigrant guidebook, "extolling the glories of California and damning Oregon with faint praise."[4]

No one could have extolled the virtues of California more convincingly than Hastings. Just his descriptions of the western region's climate were enough to stir the hearts of anyone who had struggled through a savage eastern winter of snow,

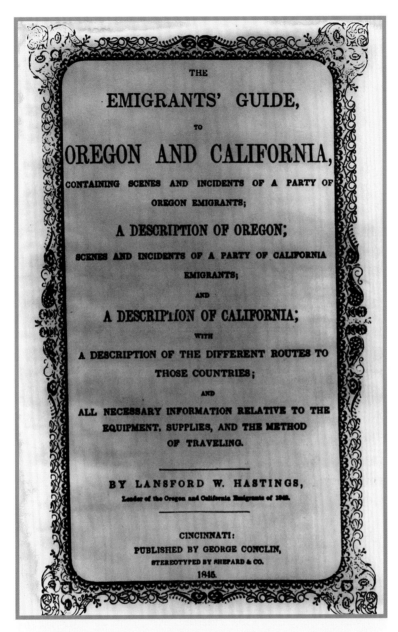

THE

EMIGRANTS' GUIDE,

TO

OREGON AND CALIFORNIA,

CONTAINING SCENES AND INCIDENTS OF A PARTY OF
OREGON EMIGRANTS;

A DESCRIPTION OF OREGON;

SCENES AND INCIDENTS OF A PARTY OF CALIFORNIA
EMIGRANTS;

AND

A DESCRIPTION OF CALIFORNIA;

WITH

A DESCRIPTION OF THE DIFFERENT ROUTES TO
THOSE COUNTRIES;

AND

ALL NECESSARY INFORMATION RELATIVE TO THE
EQUIPMENT, SUPPLIES, AND THE METHOD
OF TRAVELING.

BY LANSFORD W. HASTINGS,
Leader of the Oregon and California Emigrants of 1842.

CINCINNATI:
PUBLISHED BY GEORGE CONCLIN,
STEREOTYPED BY SHEPARD & CO.
1845.

Lansford Hastings's *The Emigrants' Guide to Oregon and California* was written to encourage people to move to California. The book described a possible route that would vastly cut down on travel time, but Hastings actually had not traveled the route himself. Hastings's guide influenced emigration to California, though not at the quantity he had hoped for.

ice, and cold or an oppressively humid summer. According to Hastings:

> The climate of the Western section [of California] is that of perpetual spring, having no excess of heat or cold, it is the most uniform and delightful. Even in the months of December and January, vegetation is in full bloom, and all nature wears a most cheering and enlivening aspect . . . you may here enjoy perennial spring, or eternal winter at your option. . . . No fires are required, at any season of the year in parlors, offices or shops, hence fuel is never required, for other than culinary purposes.[5]

For those living back East, where cutting and sawing firewood was a way of life and the seasons swung from one extreme to another, Hastings's description of California must have seemed like "paradise," indeed.

Hastings could find no end to the positives one could experience in California. Vegetables could be grown year-round. Field grains reached heights of six feet, "with stalks half an inch thick, that yielded 70 bushels to the acre with very little effort on the farmer's part."[6] The mountains were thick with timber. It almost never rained. Sickness was almost nonexistent. And there were already reports of rich deposits of gold and silver.

Those who read such boasts might have given little thought to questioning Hastings's claims. After all, he had been to California. His book included stories of his personal experiences, such as his capture by Lakota warriors, his participation in a buffalo hunt, and witnessing the death of a friend on the trail by accidental gunshot. He had walked the Oregon and California trails, had signed his name on Independence Rock, and knew everything there was to know about immigrating to the West. His book included inventories of the foods needed for the trek along the trail, arguments in favor of using oxen instead of horses or mules in pulling wagons, what tools and equipment to take on the road, and what trade items American Indians liked the most. It was all there, in Hastings's book.

To further encourage more emigrants to take the road to California, he simply shortened the route on paper. As one historian has written, "With practically no knowledge of the geography, and no investigation, he invented the Hastings Cutoff, and assured prospective emigrants that by taking it they could reach California quickly and easily."[7]

Hastings's explanation of the route was simple. Normally, wagon trains bound for California remained on the Oregon Trail until they reached Fort Hall, west of the Continental Divide and the Rocky Mountains, and north of the Great Salt Lake. Hastings included in his emigrant guide a "shortcut" of sorts, what pioneer emigrants called a "cutoff." He described a newly discovered trail running south of the Great Salt Lake. According to Hastings, emigrants bound for California would leave the Oregon Trail 200 miles short of Fort Hall, "bearing west southwest, to the Salt Lake; and thence continue down to the Bay of San Francisco."[8]

Such a viable cutoff did not really exist. Perhaps Hastings got his information through a misreading of a report by U.S. army explorer John C. Frémont. What is certain is that he had never actually taken such a route himself until 1846, and he had no real knowledge of the cutoff when he included it in his trail guide. Unfortunately, readers of Hastings's guide, including those who went west in the Donner Party, took his claim of a cutoff to California seriously.

ORGANIZING TO GO WEST

In the mid-nineteenth century, Springfield, Illinois, was a young, booming frontier town and the state's recently appointed capital. Those who lived there could see great things in its future. Having only been established 30 years earlier, Springfield sat on a wooded prairie in central Illinois, and its rich, black, fertile soil had lured pioneers from the East. The site of the frontier village had not been occupied previously, not even by American Indians, although they had frequently crossed its forests of deciduous hardwoods where hunting was good. Those who first reached the land that would one day

THE UNITED STATES AND MANIFEST DESTINY

As the Donners and the Reeds and other families prepared to go West during the 1840s, they became a part of one of the greatest movements of immigrants in U.S. history. Theirs was a feverish period of migration, an era when hundreds of thousands of people—farmers, merchants, hired hands, shop clerks, and many others—gave up their way of life and became pioneers. Such individuals were often driven by a sense of both the present and the future. What was this spirit that drove pioneers, frontiersmen, farmers, and others to claim the entire distance between the Atlantic and Pacific oceans for themselves? How did the lands that today comprise the United States come to be dominated by the United States, instead of by Great Britain, France, Spain, Russia, or by the American Indians who had arrived thousands of years earlier?

One factor that determined that the Trans-Mississippi West would be part of an "American West" was the rapid movement of migration throughout the latter decades of the eighteenth century and the early decades of the nineteenth century. When President Thomas Jefferson facilitated the purchase of the Louisiana Territory from the French in 1803, he estimated that it would take a hundred generations for the Unites States to claim and settle the entire region. In reality, it took only four. For all the decades the English colonists were content to remain settled along the Atlantic seaboard, nineteenth century East Coast residents were restless, constantly in motion, and greedy for land.

be Springfield arrived as squatters, those who did not have title to their property. They were poor pioneers—rough and resourceful vanguards—who began cutting the trees, building log cabins, planting a few acres of corn, and hunting for

Although the Louisiana Purchase did bring a vast territory of more than 800,000 square miles under the jurisdiction of the U.S. government, it was a risk to move farther west to places such as Texas, Arizona, California, or Utah—places claimed and occupied by European powers such as Great Britain and Spain. Yet, emigrants from the eastern United States seemed prepared to risk war and death to make the North American continent truly theirs.

To justify the occupation of lands that were claimed by others, there developed a philosophy that sometimes bordered on a religion. It is a concept known as "Manifest Destiny." The term was coined in 1845 by then newspaperman John O'Sullivan. To O'Sullivan, it was the destiny of the United States, determined by God, to spread itself and its democratic tendencies throughout the West, regardless of the thousands of Mexicans and American Indians living there.

Armed with the fervor of Manifest Destiny, people made their way West. Texas became a state in the Union in 1845, against the wishes of the Mexican government, which had owned Texas before the revolution led by U.S. residents of the territory. Before the end of the 1840s, the United States would fight and win a war against Mexico and lay claim to the Southwest, from Colorado to California. Great Britain would surrender its claim to the Oregon Country, prompting U.S. immigrants to stream into the fertile region by the wagonload. And when gold was discovered in the tailrace of a sawmill in California on John Sutter's ranch, nothing about the West would ever be the same again.

game as American Indians had done in the same forests for hundreds of years.

A more civilized element was added to this original number in time. By 1846, Springfield was a solid town, a good place on the prairie to call home. There were large acreages of corn and wheat, storefronts providing needed wares and household goods for the local populace, churches for the faithful, and everything else from stables to newspaper offices to hotels to banks to law offices. (One of the most successful attorneys in the frontier capital was a tall, well-liked, 37-year-old named Abraham Lincoln.) The capitol building was still in the process of being built even after nearly a decade of construction. The town also boasted a Masonic lodge, where important community leaders such as James Frazier Reed were Masons. There was a town band and a thespian society, and a reading society that met in the home of one of the town's leading families, George and Tamsen Donner. One of the town's residents, G.W. Chatterton, ran a shop offering watches, jewelry, silverware, and musical instruments. Springfield was a pleasant place, a civilized place, and its early years of pioneers eking out a living almost seemed a time long past.

But not every resident of Springfield was content to remain in the pleasant, well-established town. Even the town's leading citizens, such as James Reed and George Donner, were responding to a call to pull up their substantial and domesticated stakes and move to a land that was often described with such words as "paradise," "western heaven," and "land of opportunity." The place was California, and it seemed, in 1846, that almost everyone in the United States was hearing the same call. The lure of the West had become a fever for some. For several years, emigrants had been packing up by the thousands, loading their goods and their families in wagons, and taking to the Oregon Trail. More recently, California had become yet another important destination for those former East Coasters interested in free land. So many had gone to Oregon that, by

1846, the United States was preparing to annex the territory as its own, having pushed Great Britain out of the region. Perhaps California would be next.

Before Mexico would ever feel the pressure to abandon California to the United States, however, there would need to be thousands of U.S. citizens already living there as permanent residents. Those interested in California anxiously sought out all the information they could find on the Mexican province. They read newspaper accounts and books written by those who had already reached the promised land of California. They read government reports, including one written by the famous U.S. army officer and western explorer John C. Frémont. They also purchased guidebooks, such as the one by Lansford Hastings.

The First
"Donner Party"

Those who made up the wagon party that would become
known in history as the Donner Party came together as
a group quite accidentally. Coming together on the trail and
forming larger wagon trains out of smaller trains was not
uncommon, of course. Many times, those on the trail heard
of other parties either ahead of them or behind, and sped up
or slowed down to join them. On the trail, many considered
larger numbers to be an advantage.

THE DONNERS

A snapshot of those who made up the Donner Party, the group
that arrived at Donner Lake and became trapped, presents
a varied picture. The one they chose as their trail leader, or
captain, was a Donner, and he was just the type of individual
western immigrants liked to select for their leaders. George

Donner was a man of substance: He was of strong body but also old enough to garner respect—considered elderly at 62. An American of German descent, Donner was a prosperous farmer from Springfield, Illinois. He was thought of as a "gentle, charitable spirit."[1] He was used to moving with the frontier, having moved from North Carolina with his parents, and then on his own from Kentucky to Indiana to Illinois. He had even lived a year in Texas and was quite familiar with traveling by ox team.

He was taking three wagons west, filled with his household goods, as well as five children, all girls, the offspring of his second and third marriages. In addition, he brought in tow a herd of animals that included 12 yoke of oxen, 5 saddle horses, milk cows, beef cattle, and a dog to help keep watch over them all. His wagons were filled with articles revealing his wealth: There were gifts for American Indians and laces and silks to trade with *Californios* for land. The wagons were stuffed with books, school materials for the girls, and art supplies. Donner had dreamed of opening a young ladies' seminary in California. And although emigrants' quilts were not unique to the western trails, one of Donner's quilts was more valuable than it appeared. To hide his money, bills had been sewn into the lining. According to some reports, there may have been as much as $10,000. In addition, Donner and his wife, Tamsen, also wore money belts that held an undetermined amount of cash.

Donner's third wife, at 45 years old, was nearly 20 years younger than he. Tamsen Donner had grown up in Massachusetts and had migrated from there as a school marm. (George was her second husband.) She was thin, stood no taller than five feet, but "had a sinewy physical stamina,"[2] in addition to a sharp mind and a kind demeanor with others. Compared to most people of the United States of her day, she was very educated. With his younger wife and his five young daughters, George Donner had an air of a "gray-bearded Biblical patriarch."[3]

OTHERS FROM SPRINGFIELD

Though George Donner was selected as the party's captain and leader, there had been another contender, a friend of his—46-year-old James Frazier Reed. He was descended from Polish nobility, and Reed did have an aristocratic air. Reed was also of Scottish and Irish ancestry; in fact, he was born in Ireland, but had grown up in the United States. He was known "for quick decisions and decisive action,"[4] but despite his positive qualities, it may have been that aristocratic air that put off other members of the party, causing them to choose Donner instead.

For years, Illinois had been Reed's home. During the 1830s, he had participated in the short-lived Black Hawk War in the same company as Abraham Lincoln. Over the years, Reed had prospered, working as a merchant, railroad contractor, and furniture maker. During more recent years, his business efforts had not done so well. Despite those recent setbacks, however, Reed "was even more wealthy than Donner, or at least made more display of wealth."[5] Still, perhaps it was the opportunity to start over in the West that drew Reed to leave his home state and head out on the trail.

Like Donner, he also had three wagons, but Reed had hired men to drive them. Another paid hand did the harder jobs on the trail instead of Reed or his family members, and they also had a female cook. When the party celebrated the Fourth of July, Reed rejoiced with wine and an old brandy. Virginia Reed, his 13-year-old daughter, crossed the plains on her own pony. (Along with Virginia, there were three other siblings, as well as Reed's mother-in-law, Mrs. Sarah Keyes.) Among all the personal items Reed packed into his wagons, he included his Masonic lodge regalia, as well as a letter of introduction signed by both his congressman and the Illinois governor. While people on the western trails typically respected those of wealth and high place, they were also put off by any overt displays of prosperity. It was a mistake that Reed had made too many times.

James F. Reed and his wife, Margaret, pose in a photo taken in the 1850s. Reed organized a group and spent nearly a year preparing for the journey to California. Reed and his family left much of the documentary evidence of the excursion through diaries, letters, and interviews and memoirs written afterward.

George and Tamsen Donner and their daughters were not the only Donners in the party. George's older brother, Jacob, was also traveling with his wife, Elizabeth, and her two older sons from a previous marriage, Solomon and William. There were another five Donner children, age 9 and under. The Jacob Donner family's relationship with the other Donners was complicated, since George's deceased second wife was the sister of Elizabeth Donner. Jacob was "industrious and kindly, but age was telling on him."[6] While George was still in good form, Jacob, in his mid-sixties, was not in the best of health.

Traveling with the Donners and Reeds were several young men, also from Springfield, who are remembered by name but who would play relatively insignificant roles in the events that would make the Donner Party gruesomely famous. They included Milt Elliott, Walter Herron, James Smith, and Baylis Williams, all of whom traveled and worked for the Donners. With the Reeds were Noah James, Samuel Shoemaker, and John Denton.

PREPARING TO LEAVE THEIR HOMES

Those Springfield residents who packed up for the West did not do so haphazardly. Many months of planning preceded the move. George Donner, for example, had put his farm up for sale back in September 1845, land that included 240 acres with peach, pear, and apple trees and a large farmhouse with two chimneys. Tamsen Donner spent the winter of 1845 to 1846 sewing clothing for the trek along the western trail. In March 1846, George ran an advertisement in a local paper, *The Sangamo Journal*, calling for others to join him and his family on a trip to California—not as fellow emigrants, but as hired hands:

> WESTWARD HO! FOR OREGON AND CALIFORNIA. Who wants to go to California without costing them anything? As many as eight young men, of good character, who can drive an ox team, will be accommodated by gentlemen who will leave this vicinity about the first of April. Come boys! You can have as much land as you want without costing you any thing. The government of California gives tracts of land to persons who have to move there.[7]

In the end, the advertisement only drummed up four teamsters for George and his older brother, Jacob.

As the weeks approached the scheduled departure time, the Donner family's three wagons were prepared for the trail following advice they had read about in Hastings's guidebook. The first wagon was filled with trade goods suggested by Hastings, including bolts of cotton cloth, flannels, brightly colored handkerchiefs, glass beads, small mirrors, necklaces, and rings—all for barter with American Indians. For the *Californios* (residents of modern-day California who were of Spanish or Mexican descent), the Donners included more expensive textiles, such as laces, muslins, silks, and satins. That first wagon also included such items as farm equipment, furniture, and Tamsen's school and art supplies. In all, the first wagon included all kinds of items the Donners would not need until they reached California.

The second wagon included nearly everything they would need on a daily basis, including food, clothing, tools for the trail, and camping equipment. Again, Hastings's trail guide had led the Donners in making their plans. The third wagon had been designed to provide their lodging. This specially designed wagon also included feed boxes attached to the rear for the family's two favorite saddle horses.

On April 15, the Donners were fully packed and ready to head to the rendezvous site at the edge of town. There they met the Reeds with their three wagons. These wagons were unlike any other wagons on the Oregon Trail during the 1840s; Reed had custom designed them, and they were symbols of how to go West in style. The wagon the family would travel in "was a double-decker, with comfortable spring seats on the lower level and regular bunks on the upper level, much like a modern camper."[8] Reed had thought of everything. His family would not suffer from the cold, for he had a sheet-iron stove built into his family wagon to provide heat. For nearly everyone else on the trail, the practice was to sleep outside on the ground. Virginia Reed wrote about the stove: "Mornings and evenings we could make a fire and warm the wagon up for Grandma."[9] The Reed wagon even included a set of folding steps the family could use to enter the wagon, eliminating the commonplace

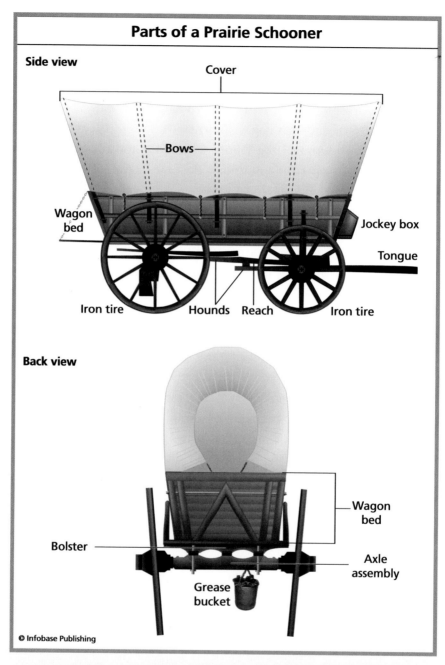

Parts of a Prairie Schooner

Side view

Cover

Bows

Wagon bed

Jockey box

Tongue

Iron tire   Hounds   Reach   Iron tire

Back view

Wagon bed

Bolster

Axle assembly

Grease bucket

© Infobase Publishing

Covered wagons were used primarily to transport goods. Up to four oxen would pull the wagon while the father would drive the oxen by walking beside the wagon. Pioneers preferred to walk behind the wagon unless they had horses to ride, since the roads were rough and the wagons had no suspension. Small children, the elderly, and the sick or injured rode inside.

need to climb in over the top edge of the wagon box. It was really more like a fancy stagecoach than a wagon. There was even a five-foot-tall mirror opposite the wagon's entrance door, a present from Margaret Reed's female friends, "so that she would not forget her good looks on the plains."[10] Reed had planned the wagon with a place for everything from toys to "a small library of select books, knowing such things were scarce in a new country."[11] The Reed family wagon was so fancy that the oldest daughter, Virginia, described it as "the Pioneer Palace Car." She said, "Our wagon was so comfortable that mama could sit reading and chatting with the little ones and almost forget she was crossing the plains."[12] Four yoke of oxen (a total of eight animals) were required to pull the oversized wagon.

Before these families left Springfield for good, several friends and family members visited them. The Reeds' reading society associates came out on horseback to wish them well. According to some stories, Mary Todd Lincoln also stopped by to wish her neighbors a safe trip. Her husband, Abraham, was out of town on a court case. Virginia Reed noted these many good-byes in her diary. As the moment of actual departure from Springfield arrived, she wrote how her mother, "who had kept up so bravely was now over come with greafe and had to be almost carried out of the house."[13]

ON THE TRAIL

The party leaving Springfield included the two extended Donner families, plus the Reeds, with the three families taking up nine wagons. Adding the number of employees hired by both families, the party included 32 people. From Illinois, they set out for neighboring Missouri, setting a leisurely pace, generally following the Missouri River. They faced few significant problems on this leg of their western trek, except for the rains. Thunderstorms plagued the group, and mud was a constant challenge for humans, animals, and wagons alike.

Through these early weeks on the trail, the participants fell into a daily routine, one that would serve them on their cross-country trek. Each night, the party camped along the Missouri River or by some nearby stream. Nearly everyone over the age of five had regular chores. The women usually did the cooking, laundering, sewing and mending, and watching after the children. The men took care of the animals, hunting, and wagon maintenance. Children might handle light chores, including getting out the dishes for a meal, fetching water, helping with food preparation, or a variety of other duties. Nearly everyone had a sense of responsibility.

After 300 miles on the road, the Donners and Reeds reached their first major stop, which for many emigrant parties traveling on the Oregon Trail was actually a jumping-off place: the bustling trail center town of Independence, Missouri. The oxen had set a pace of 10 to 12 miles a day, arriving on May 10. Although the parties were not alarmed, they were actually already running slightly behind the normal schedule for heading out on the Oregon Trail, which, from Independence, was May 1. As the Donners and Reeds knew from their reading of Hastings's trail guide, getting on the western trail in a timely fashion was crucial and could easily determine a wagon party's success or failure in reaching its ultimate goal in California or Oregon. Those who got a later start sometimes found it difficult to find adequate grass for the livestock, since earlier wagon train teams would have eaten the grass down too short. If a party was headed to California, getting an early enough start was important since winter snows could fall early in the mountains. Most veterans of the trail preached that the Sierra Nevada could be safely crossed, generally, by September. If a party hit the mountains as late as October, success was uncertain. Already, the party from Springfield was late on the trail.

Wisely, the Donners and Reeds decided not to linger long in Independence. Tamsen Donner described their plans in a letter to a sister in Massachusetts: "It is supposed there will be

7,000 wagons will start from this place this season. We go to California, to the bay of San Francisco. It is a four months trip. I am willing to go & have no doubt it will be an advantage to our children & to us."[14]

JOINING THE RUSSELL TRAIN

The party from Springfield was informed that a large party of wagons was waiting to the west along Wakarusa Creek in Kansas for late wagon trains to join them. If the Springfield emigrants hurried, they might catch up to the others. By May 12, the Donners and Reeds were on the trail. By the time they reached Wakarusa Creek, the others had left already, but the Donners and Reeds finally overtook them at Soldier Creek after a few days on the trail. It would fall to Reed to talk to the other wagon train's leader, Colonel William H. Russell, to get permission to join his party. Armed with his letter from both his congressman and the governor of Illinois, Reed convinced Russell to welcome them all. Just prior to joining the Russell train, the Donner-Reed group had already hired a young Hispanic man, a herder named Antoine.

Russell's group included several important emigrants. Russell himself, originally from Kentucky, had served as secretary to Henry Clay, one of the most famous senators of the first half of the nineteenth century. Out in Missouri, Russell had managed to snag an appointment as a U.S. marshal. There was also a former Missouri governor in the group, Lillburn Boggs, who was famous for helping to drive the Mormons from his state a few years earlier. Another emigrant, Jessy Quinn Thornton, was a fellow Illinoisan, a lawyer who was good friends with one of the state's senators, Stephen A. Douglas, whom Reed's friend, Abraham Lincoln, would run against for senator in 1858.

After Russell signed on the Donners and Reeds, he took an inventory of the enlarged wagon train for which he was responsible. It included 72 wagons, 130 men, 65 women, a whopping

125 children, and 710 cattle, oxen, and horses. Between them all, these emigrants carried 155 guns (most of them rifles) and 104 pistols. Their inventory of food included nearly 70,000 pounds of flour and more than 40,000 pounds of bacon, both staples on the western trail.

WAR ON THE HORIZON

As the Donners, Reeds, and others prepared to set out on the Oregon Trail bound for the West, they did not know that events taking place between Mexico and the United States would soon have an impact on their future. These two nations were preparing to go to war.

Throughout much of the first half of the nineteenth century, the United States's drive to dominate the vast open lands of the Trans-Mississippi West, as well as the West, seemed to know no limits. During the 1840s, the United States went to war with Mexico to acquire additional territory that the Mexican government had no intentions of surrendering. The Mexican-American War was a conflict created by the United States.

The primary antagonist was President James K. Polk, who was elected in 1844 on a platform that promised the annexation of both the Oregon Country and Texas. The latter became a state in 1845, and Polk successfully negotiated for Oregon under a 1846 treaty. As an expansionist president, he intended to acquire even more territory than this. During the spring of 1846, relations between Mexico and the United States deteriorated dramatically. There was a controversy over the U.S. acquisition of Oregon and the annexation of Texas as a U.S. state. (Texas had once been a part of Mexico, but a U.S.-inspired and led revolution during the mid-1830s had succeeded in wresting Texas from Mexican control.) When the United States claimed Texas to include the land

This enlarged wagon train hit the trail on May 16. With so many wagons, the group was organized to move out in units. On the trail, rumors soon circulated: The local American Indians, the Kansa, were looking for whites to attack. Somewhere ahead on the trail, armed bands of Mormons were lying in wait, ready

north of the Rio Grande, the Mexicans were furious. The Mexican government had never recognized the Rio Grande as the western boundary of the Republic of Texas, but rather, the Nueces River.

In June 1845, just months after the annexation of Texas, President Polk sent General Zachary Taylor into Texas, where, by October, Taylor led U.S. forces to the northern bank of the Rio Grande as a direct challenge to Mexican forces. By doing so, Polk intended to stir up a war. At the same time he sent Taylor to the Rio Grande, Polk secretly dispatched U.S. Navy vessels to Mexican-controlled California. The president also sent instructions to the U.S. envoy in Monterey, Thomas Larkin, that the United States would welcome a revolt of Californians against the Mexican government. On another front, Polk sent a negotiator to Mexico City to offer to buy the lands from California to Texas for $25 million. If that failed, the representative was to offer to pay to establish the Rio Grande as the Texas border.

Envoy John Slidell was not even given an audience with Mexican officials, who were not interested in any such offer from the United States. An angry Polk responded to the Mexican rebuff by ordering General Taylor and his men to cross the Nueces and take up positions along the banks of the Rio Grande in defiance of the Mexicans. In the battle of Palo Alto in April 1846, Mexican troops attacked the U.S. military presence, prompting Polk to appeal to Congress for a declaration of war.

to raid wagon trains in retaliation for having been driven out of Missouri. There were scares involving British army officers who were encouraging American Indian raids against wagon parties. Rumors of war with Mexico were circulating, too, a scare that mattered to any and all who were headed to California. Once the train got underway, however, most of these stories faded away as the realities of the trail loomed ahead.

Progress on
the Trail

Cutting northwest across the open prairies of Kansas was, for many on the trail, "like an extended picnic."[1] The trail was friendly there, offering few real challenges. Spring flowers were in bloom, the weather was relatively pleasant, and the fields were green with the various grasses of the plains.

For the Reeds, however, tragedy struck on May 29 near today's Alcove Springs, Kansas, when Sarah Keyes, Margaret Reed's mother, died. The elderly Keyes, about 70 years old, had been in declining health for a year or so, brought on by consumption (called tuberculosis today). The train stopped long enough for the men to fashion a coffin out of a felled cottonwood tree and bury her beneath a large oak tree on the banks of the Big Blue River. Family members placed a "head stone and had her name cut on it and the date and yere [year]."[2] Of her grandmother's passing, Virginia Reed wrote, "We buried her verry decent We made a nete [neat] coffin and buried her under a tree we had a head stone and had her name cutonit. . . We miss her verry much evry time we come in the wagon we look up at the bed for her."[3] Although her death was an emotional loss for the Reed family, Sarah Keyes would be spared the horrors that lay on the opposite end of the trail that stretched ahead of them.

WAGONS ACROSS NEBRASKA

The party pushed on, reaching Nebraska by early June. For many emigrants, these were halcyon days, spent enjoying nature and the beauty of the Great Plains. Tamsen Donner described in a letter all the wonderful experiences of the trail:

> Our cattle are in good order . . . Our milch cows have been of great service, indeed. They have been of more advantage than our meat. We have plenty of butter and milk . . . Buffaloes show themselves frequently. We have found the wild tulip, the primrose, the lupine, the eardrop, the larkspur, and creeping hollyhock, and a beautiful flower resembling the bloom of the beech tree, but in bunches as large as a small sugar-loaf, and of every variety of shade, to red and green.[4]

The region was similar to Kansas, relatively flat and almost treeless, with streams cutting across the path of the western emigrants.

Soon, however, the calm was broken when the first fights between party members broke out. Fists flew between a pair of ox teamsters during a heavy rainfall. The two young men had simply lost their tempers, and, even though little damage was done during the short-lived outburst, the quarrel signaled that "the spirit of goodwill, of cooperation, of loyalty to each other was eroding."[5] In the future, the wagon train divided into smaller units. One additional reason for this was the varied paces of the wagons. Those with faster oxen often ran ahead of the rest of the party. During any given day crossing Nebraska, "families passed and repassed each other dozens of times, sometimes camping together and sometimes with strangers."[6]

Today, this leg of the Oregon Trail is paralleled by a major interstate that passes east to west across Nebraska, Highway 80. This same route is crossed repeatedly by the Platte River, a shallow basin that meanders across the Great Plains landscape, usually running shallow and wide. The wagon party reached the Platte at Fort Kearney. Following the river, the emigrants reached the natural rock formations that every pioneer on the trail looked for to mark his or her progress, including Chimney Rock, Courthouse Rock, and Scott's Bluff, all in western Nebraska. At Chimney Rock, Virginia Reed carved her father's name into the stone. As they passed Scott's Bluff, some in the party thought the rock ridges looked like an abandoned city out of *The Arabian Nights.* Having been on the trail from Independence for five weeks now, Tamsen Donner wrote to her sister: "I never could have believed we could have traveled so far with so little difficulty."[7]

INTO WYOMING

Passing into modern-day Wyoming, the party reached the next important stop on the trail, Fort Laramie. It was there that the emigrants found their first critic of Lansford Hastings: James Clyman, a famous former mountain man and western explorer. Clyman gave a stern warning not to follow the Hastings Cutoff. "I told Reed to take the regular wagon track and never leave it," he explained later. "[I]t is barely possible to get through if you follow it—and maybe impossible if you don't. I told him about the great desert and the roughness of the Sierra, and that a straight route might turn out to be impracticable."[8] Clyman knew all too well the difficulties of Hastings Cutoff. He had crossed the route with Hastings himself in 1846. Hastings even admitted to Clyman that "the route was well-nigh impassable for wagons."[9] Unfortunately,

JAMES CLYMAN

Trapper, explorer and California pioneer. One of the four men who circumnavigated Great Salt Lake in 1825

FROM "JAMES CLYMAN," CALIFORNIA HISTORICAL SOCIETY
SPECIAL PUBLICATION NO. 3

James Clyman was an experienced, well-respected mountain man and beaver trapper. In 1846, on his way back to Missouri after traveling through western Oregon and California, he followed a path similar to the supposed Hastings Cutoff. Later, he spent a night talking with the Donner Party and warned them not to take that route.

Reed did not listen to Clyman, a curious response considering the relationship between the two men. Reed and Clyman had known one another for years, having both fought in the Black Hawk War back in the 1830s. Friend or not, though, Reed was intent on following Hastings's advice, and the lure of cutting off several hundred miles from the trail ahead meant more to him than advice from an old friend.

At the fort, the emigrants had seen some of their first American Indians up close. Several Lakota had been there, having been convinced by the fort's manager to abandon their plans to engage in raiding on the trail. One Lakota chief was determined to purchase both Virginia Reed and her pony. He was an important leader and he offered several "Indian ponies, piles of hides, and . . . an old U.S. Army jacket with brass buttons."[10] Virginia's father politely refused to sell either his 13-year-old daughter or the horse. To make certain his daughter was safe after they set off, Reed had Virginia ride in the wagon until they were a distance from the fort.

At this point in the trek, the Donners and Reeds had little to concern them. They were running a week behind, but their progress was steady and few problems plagued their advance. River crossings were a constant danger, but caution was always the watchword. They were, of course, experiencing the usual challenges of the trail, including bad hygiene caused by a lack of opportunity to keep clothes clean or to bathe. The farther west they pushed, diarrhea became a regular problem. The western water was so alkali-heavy that it worked as a natural laxative. The emigrants also battled trail dust, and their wagon parts became loose due to the arid environment, but these were the circumstances of the trail to which no one was exempt.

The calendar read early July when the party reached Independence Rock a week later than trail guides suggested. (The optimum date was the Fourth of July, Independence Day.)

On July 4, James Reed celebrated with a special bottle of liquor, as described by Virginia:

> We selabrated the 4 of July on plat at bever criek several of the Gentemen in Springfield gave paw a botel of licker and said it shouden be opend tell the 4 day of July and paw was to look to the east and drink it and thay was to look to the West an drink it at 12 oclock paw treted the company and we all had some leminade.[11]

AN EXPANDED PARTY

Still more wagons joined the party. One of the largest families was the Murphy family from Tennessee. The center of the family was the elderly Lavina Murphy, a widow, who traveled with her seven children. Two were married, and their husbands, William Foster and William Pike, were part of their family circle, along with several children. All in all, the Murphy clan numbered 13 people. Unlike the Donners and Reeds, they were simple, common people with no real wealth.

Another family head was William Eddy, joined by his wife, Eleanor, and their two young children, James and Margaret. Eddy was from Belleville, Illinois, and had worked as a carriagemaker. He was a strong fellow, a tough and energetic worker. He also proved to be the party's best hunter and "the most skilled in the arts of the frontiersman."[12]

These families—the Donners, the Reeds, the Murphys, and the Eddys—appear to have seen themselves as the backbone of the wagon party and may "have looked upon the other families as foreigners."[13] The Breens, for one, were an Irish family. Even though they had lived in the United States for two years before the summer of 1846, "the brogue was still on [their] lips."[14] Being Irish was often considered a negative in nineteenth-century America, and the prejudiced stereotype of all Irish immigrants was of people who were dirty, lazy, and uneducated, not to mention drinkers, brawlers, and Catholics.

Patrick Breen, the family patriarch, did not fit the mold. He was literate and even kept a diary of the trip. He and his family came from Iowa, where he had owned a farm. He was no poor dirt farmer, either, for the Breens traveled with three wagons, just like the Donners and Reeds. Along with the Breens was a young man named Patrick Dolan, who entertained the emigrants with his singing and Irish jigs.

There were others, Germans, including the Kesebergs and Wolfingers, who had immigrated to the United States just a few years earlier and were reasonably well off. Mrs. Wolfinger wore her best jewelry even on the trail, a practice that would not serve her well on her way west. A Belgian-American named Hardkoop traveled with the Kesebergs, as well as a teamster named "Dutch Charley" Burger. Two additional Germans, Joseph Reinhardt and Augustus Spitzer were with the Kesebergs, traveling together in the same wagon. The Donners had picked up some additional passengers themselves, including young Luke Halloran and Charles T. Stanton.

Even as the party generally welcomed these new additions, the Springfield members of the train "kept a certain psychological distance" from the other emigrants.[15] Lewis Keseberg was a particular problem, as it soon came out that he beat his wife. Keseberg would create new issues for the wagon train members, especially James Reed. As Tamsen Donner wrote: "We have some of the best people in our company and some, too, that are not so good."[16]

Traveling the Oregon Trail was rarely about emigrants making strong friendships with everyone in their wagon party. It was about getting to one's destination. So, in most cases, pioneers simply tried to overlook their fellow travelers' shortcomings and make the best of it. After all, they were in a shared experience by necessity, and cooperation was crucial to a wagon train's ultimate success. This sort of cooperation, however, was not always possible.

THE ROAD TO THE CUTOFF

From the beginning, the Reed and Donner families had planned on taking Hastings Cutoff. Despite warnings from others, such as James Clyman, they remained firm in their intentions since they believed they could make up their time on the trail by taking this supposed shortcut. Then, as the party moved past Independence Rock and covered the next 20 miles to Sweetwater River, they met yet another trail traveler who had an opinion about Hastings Cutoff. This man's opinion came straight from Hastings himself.

The traveler, Wales Bonney, was a young family man taking the trail alone back East to fetch his family. He had immigrated to Oregon the previous year. Since traveling alone was dangerous, Bonney had made a practice of hiding by day with his horse in any ravine that provided him cover, and then traveling by night. He and Hastings had met earlier on the trail, and Hastings had given Bonney a letter to show to all emigrants he encountered on his trek back East. The gist of the missive was clear: Mexican authorities were organizing to turn back U.S. emigrants trying to enter California. Therefore, Hastings warned, all parties should enter California in as large a wagon train as possible to be able to better defend against Mexican attack. He also suggested strongly that they take his cutoff to shorten their time on the trail and conserve their physical strength. In addition, the letter stated that Hastings would wait at Fort Bridger and personally lead any emigrants along his cutoff. This only confirmed the confidence of the Springfield party in taking Hastings Cutoff when the moment came.

Soon, the party reached South Pass, the wide opening in the Rocky Mountains that allowed wagons to push through and across the mountainous spine of North America's Continental Divide. West of the divide, the rivers flow westward. It was a key mile marker on the trail and the emigrants were surprised at how wide the pass opened up before them. The pass itself was nearly level and stretched across a width of almost 20

The Green River, which is about 730 miles long and runs through three states (Wyoming, Colorado, and Utah), was a main route for emigrants who made their way west from the 1840s to the 1860s. Nearly all of the primary trails had to cross the Green River at some point. Above is the Green River and Steamboat Rock in Colorado.

miles. Beyond South Pass, the emigrant train began its gradual descent toward the Sandy River. During the crossing at Dry Sandy Creek (a small stream that is a tributary of the Little Sandy River), both Donner men and James Reed lost a total of five oxen from alkali water poisoning. Several more oxen died a day later at Little Sandy River.

The Little Sandy River was a crossroads for the party. The stream flowed into the Big Sandy River, which was a tributary

TWO MEN ON A COLLISION COURSE

As they continued along the Oregon Trail, following the Platte River in the summer of 1846, the members of the Donner Party might have found it difficult to imagine the fate that lay ahead for them in the Far West. Their days in Nebraska and Wyoming were not perfect by any stretch, but the problems they faced were typical for the trail. Struggling to get along with fellow party members was as normal on the Oregon Trail as buffalo chips and prairie dogs.

Personal clashes along the trail would, however, prove to work against the party's fate when circumstances became unbearable and dangerous. Among the most antagonistic of relationships was that between Lewis Keseberg and James Reed. They were two men cut from different bolts of cloth. Reed's airs and aristocratic ways constantly put off Keseberg. The German-American was simple in his ways and rough, especially with his wife. It seems he was fond of beating his spouse, a practice that Reed abhorred and promised to punish him for if given the opportunity.

Along the trail, one incident stands out for driving a permanent wedge of hatred between the two men. While traveling along the Platte, the wagon train passed a Lakota burial site. It seems that Keseberg and a fellow German left the trail long enough to rob the gravesite, including removing the bison robes wrapped around the deceased American Indian man's body. Reed was appalled at the act of defilement and approached Keseberg directly. The Illinoisan gave him a threatening tongue-lashing and ordered him to return the pilfered items.

Reed's anger was extremely justified. Not only was grave robbing morally wrong, but also the Lakota in the region would have taken the desecration of one of their burial sites as an insult that might have led them to take revenge. The incident would permanently put bad blood between Reed and Keseberg.

of the Green River. Pioneers would follow these streams to Fort Bridger on the main trail. At Little Sandy Creek, the Russell wagon train stopped and camped for the night on Sunday, July 19. It would be the last encampment for the entire train. The following day, the majority of the train, including those bound for Oregon and many headed for California, took the Greenwood Cutoff, which had just been discovered the previous year by mountain man Caleb Greenwood. This would eliminate 100 miles of the older trail, pass through the Forty-Mile Desert, and ultimately lead to Fort Hall. This was a tried and true route, and the main party guide was not convinced about Hastings Cutoff.

The Reeds, Donners, and several others bade good-bye to the main party, still intending to take their planned route. The separation included well-wishing among both groups and some teary good-byes. As for Tamsen Donner, perhaps she knew more than the rest of her party. She immediately became, according to Jessy Thornton, "gloomy, sad, and dispirited, in view of the fact, that her husband and others, could think for a moment of leaving the old road and confide in the statement of a man of whom they knew nothing, but who was probably some selfish adventurer."[17]

Nearly everyone else in this party who now bore to the left on the new trail was excited about their decision. They were certain the trail before them represented their best hope of making up for lost time and reaching California before the snows fell. Following the Little Sandy, Fort Bridger lay somewhere in the great distance.

A Badly
Advised Road

Tamsen Donner was not the only member of the party with doubts about following Hastings Cutoff. One of the Donners' hired hands, a teamster named Hiram Miller, chose to leave his employer and continue along the trail with the group headed to Fort Hall.

Before taking the left cutoff, the Donner Party did take a vote, but the women were not allowed to cast ballots, even though the older boys were allowed a ballot. Then, once the decision was made to follow the route lauded by Hastings and encouraged by James Reed, the party took another vote, this time for a new trail captain. This is when the grandfatherly George Donner, whom almost everyone was by then referring to as "Uncle George," took leadership. From this point on, this wagon train would be forever remembered as the Donner Party.

Emigrants traveling west passed many forts along the way. Some were fur trading posts where emigrants traded goods with American Indians and sent letters home to loved ones. Later, Congress approved the construction of military forts and a special regiment of riflemen to man them to ensure the safety of the travelers. This painting shows the interior of Fort Laramie, one of the most famous forts in the American West.

DOWN THE LITTLE SANDY

It was late July before the Donner Party reached Fort Bridger in the southwest region of modern-day Wyoming. They had traveled 18 miles that day. The fort was situated within a lush mountain meadow on Black's Fork, a tributary of the Green River. It was not a grand stop on the trail, unlike Fort Laramie. Bridger was little more than "two large, ill-kept log cabins at either end of a palisaded corral."[1]

Lansford Hastings was supposed to be at the fort waiting, but he was not present, having already left with a group of 86 wagons. It was late in the season, and he did not think he could wait any longer. He had left instructions with Jim Bridger, the fort's namesake, to send on any late arrivals. Bridger and another former mountain man and partner at the fort, Louis Vasquez, were reassuring about continuing along the cutoff. Bridger even described the trail ahead as "a fine level road, with plenty of water and grass."[2]

The truth was Bridger knew better than this; however, he had been losing business at his fort since the opening of the Greenwood Cutoff a couple of years earlier. There are also indications that Hastings may have paid Bridger and Vasquez to speak confidently of his route. Vasquez, in fact, held letters he had received from Reed's friend Edwin Bryant. Reed and Bryant had traveled together earlier on the trail, but Bryant had pushed far ahead with each passing week. Bryant's letters warned Reed and his party not to take the cutoff any farther. Bryant had managed to take the cutoff with a group using mules, but no wagons. As he stated in his warning: "We could afford to hazard experiments, and make explorations. They [those with wagons and families] could not."[3] Vasquez never gave the letters to Reed.

As for Reed, he had no insight that Bridger and Vasquez did not have his party's best interests in mind. In a letter he wrote for the pages of his hometown newspaper, *The Sangamo Journal*, Reed described Bridger and Vasquez as "two very excellent and accommodating gentlemen."[4] Bridger informed Reed that his party should stay on the trail and that they were only 700 miles from Sutter's Fort in San Francisco Valley. Bridger said the wagon party could reach the fort in seven weeks, which would place their arrival at the back end of October, the month the mountain snows began to fall. Both men told the Donner Party that the desert south of the Great Salt Lake was "the only bad part."[5]

The Donner Party only remained at Fort Bridger for three days, which allowed time to rest the oxen and do repairs on their wagons, which had taken a beating since leaving Fort Laramie. In the meantime, others joined the Donner Party, including a young teamster named Jean-Baptiste Trubode, who would replace Hiram Miller. There was also a new Missouri family of three, the McCutchens. The head, William McCutchen, stood 6 feet 6 inches tall and often quoted from Shakespeare. His family wagon was in no shape to continue traveling, but George Donner said the train could make room for them. With the addition of the McCutchen family, the Donner Party now included five nursing babies and 26 children under the age of 12. With these new additions to their party, the emigrants left Fort Bridger on July 31 with 20 wagons. The road ahead of them could not have been more uncertain.

Although Bridger had assured the Donner Party of a "fine level road," they were immediately in the midst of a rough crossing, including steep grades, through the Wyoming badlands. The landscape was both desolate and ethereal. Great rock formations loomed along their path, and the wagons dipped into thin ravines and steep hillsides, where they were fortunate to remain upright. Some places on the trail were so rocky, "the clatter of their wheels resounded for miles."[6] They passed natural soda springs and springs where iron deposits colored the water a dirty red. The party was approaching the Wasatch Range of mountains. Four days out of Bridger, the party reached the Red Fork of the Weber River, which would lead them to the south banks of the Great Salt Lake. The emigrants were relieved when they rolled their wagons into a wide mountain meadow running along the Weber (in modern-day Utah).

It was there on August 6 that they found an ominous sign along the road, left behind by Hastings himself. It was a note attached to a bush, addressed to all parties following the trail behind him. The message was a warning: He and his party of wagons had encountered a most difficult leg of the cutoff, and Hastings was strongly suggesting that any wagon train following him wait until he got his wagon train through the Sierra, then he would come back and lead anyone waiting along the trail. He also asked that any parties following him send a messenger forward to let him know that they were waiting.

Immediately, nearly everyone in the Donner Party knew that Hastings had led the group astray and could not be trusted. Three riders, including Reed, went ahead to reach him, but when they found Hastings on the trail, he refused to leave the wagon train he was leading. He had already lost one wagon that had slid, along with its draught animals, off a cliff 75 feet high.

Hastings took Reed up on a nearby mountaintop, where he showed Reed the basic route of the trail ahead, but he would not and could not provide any additional help. After being gone for four days, Reed returned to the main train alone, having borrowed a fresh horse from Hastings's train, and reported on his meeting. The Donner Party was on their own.

There they were, in hostile Weber Canyon, with no further hope of receiving outside, expert help. It was too late to turn back to the main trail, so they pushed forward. Advance was excruciating, as the Donner Party had to use block and tackle to winch wagons up hillsides, just as the Hastings wagon train had already done along the same leg of the cutoff. They were moving in the midst of some of the roughest landscape in the entire Far West, practically forced to clear their own trail in certain places. They moved so slowly that they were surprised when another small train of three wagons caught up with them. Franklin Graves and his family—13 people in all—were farmers from Illinois. The main party was excited when it saw that the Graves family included four strong, young men who could lend a further hand in their advance through the harsh landscape. These were the last additions to the Donner Party, a total of 87 emigrants traveling in 23 wagons. After the addition of the Graves, the other two scouts who had reached Hastings's train returned. They had become lost on their return trip, and their food supplies ran so low they had almost killed their horses.

SLOW PROGRESS

The party pushed onward, because progress or perish were their only options. They worked endlessly, felling trees, prying giant boulders from their path, but progress was slow, no more than two miles a day sometimes. At places, the hills were so steep that everyone's oxen had to be hitched to a single wagon to make it up the forbidding incline; then the process was repeated for a second, and then third wagon, until all 23 had mastered the hill.

Everyone's nerves were stretched. For some, James Reed was becoming unbearable. He had been the party's most vociferous advocate of Hastings Cutoff. Yet, even as the train crept along, Reed did not lend much of an active hand in the struggle. As one of the Graves boys later wrote: "Reed, being an aristocratic fellow, was above working, so he had hired hands to drive his teams and he gave orders, although no one paid much attention to him . . . the company humored him a good deal."[7] There would be problems later between Reed and several of his fellow emigrants.

After weeks of grueling, backbreaking labor, the Donner Party reached the Valley of the Great Salt Lake. The party had taken 18 days to cover less than 40 miles—the distance from the site of Hastings's note on a lonely western shrub until they arrived on the nearly level plains south of the lake. It was a leg of the trail they had planned on taking no more than a week to cover. The plain along the lake was a respite, featuring thick grass for the animals and good water in nearby springs. Tired as they all were, including the animals, the party did not stop to rest. It was late August, and California and its forbidding Sierra Nevada range were still hundreds of miles to the west.

Soon after their arrival along the Great Salt Lake, a member of their party, Luke Halloran died. The death was not from the rigors of the trail directly, but rather from consumption. Halloran was the man whom George and Tamsen Donner had picked up along the trail following the Little Sandy River. His

Emigrants were at the mercy of extreme weather, in constant fear of being attacked by both humans and wild animals, and drinking water was hard to find. Diseases were the most deadly threat posed to the pioneers. For miles travelers encountered the graveyards of fellow pioneers, sometimes holding the bodies of entire families. Pictured is a pioneer gravesite on the Oregon Trail near Gering, Nebraska.

horse had given out, and he was unable to go on due to his declining health, causing his earlier wagon train to leave him. Tamsen had nursed him through the weeks prior to his death, and he died with his head on her lap. Before he died, he left his belongings to the Donners, including his horse and tack gear, and an old, battered trunk. With his passing, George and Tamsen opened the trunk, where they found the surprise of their lives. The young consumptive had been carrying $1,500 in gold coins. The trunk also held "the full regalia of a Master Mason."[8]

Several in the emigrant train donated wooden planks to construct a coffin. After moving the wagons a few more miles along the trail to a better campsite, they held a funeral. Those among their number who were themselves Masons conducted a funeral that included the ceremonial rites of the order. The young Halloran, who had left Missouri bound for California, "an invalid in search of health,"[9] was buried in a marsh. Next to his was another grave belonging to an unknown victim of the Hastings wagon train ahead of them.

In respect for Halloran, the party did not travel on the day he was buried. On the following day, August 27, the train was moving again. Although the landscape was flat and more hospitable than mountains or rocky creek beds, the party was approaching a desert. Nothing lay on the horizon ahead of them, just a range of mountains off to their left. It was a land of jackrabbits and lizards, with no shade from the sun. The springs they reached offered only trickles of water.

They were still following the tracks of Hastings's wagon train. Hastings had promised the desert crossing would take no more than a day and a night. But Tamsen Donner soon found a piece of board with tattered pieces of paper tacked to it. Other pieces of paper lay about the same site. After piecing the mysterious scraps together, Tamsen could read their discouraging, yet uncertain message: "2 days—2 nights—hard driving—cross desert—water."[10]

INTO THE DESERT

The next day was August 30, and an unknown distance of desert lay in front of them. The party had reached a site with a good spring and thick grasses. John Breen thought the site was so good, "we should have wintered there."[11] But on September 1, with their water barrels filled and bundles of grass cut and stored for their animals, the Donner Party continued on.

Everyone knew they had not packed enough water; to do so to cover two days of desert travel was impossible. Water weighs 8 pounds a gallon, and most wagons could not carry more than 30 gallons. One ox alone could consume 20 gallons in a day, so rationing water was their only hope.

A REGION IN TURMOIL

Before the Mexican-American War, which delivered California into the hands of the U.S. government, the great coastal region was home to dozens of small nations of American Indians, about 50,000 people, and 7,000 *Californios*, or Spanish-speaking Mexicans, many of whom descended from families that had lived in California since the late 1700s. In just a few years, by 1850, California would become a U.S. state. This great change occurred when gold was discovered in the rivers west of the Sierra Nevada.

Before the coming of the war, some people in the United States had schemed to separate California from Mexican control. Lansford Hastings, for one, had decided a few years earlier that Mexican control of California was tenuous and he had campaigned to encourage more people to leave the East and move to California. This would presumably turn the tide away from Mexican provincial control to one of U.S. dominance in the region.

The first serious U.S. challenge to Mexican authority in California took place in June 1846, as the Donners and their comrades were moving along the Oregon Trail. It occurred when a band of U.S. citizens joined forces at Sonoma (north of present-day San Francisco), calling for independence from Mexico. They created an emblem for their revolution, a flag featuring an image of a bear, giving the insurrection the name of the Bear Flag Revolt.

One of the revolt's leaders was an explorer and U.S. army officer, John C. Frémont. He was on an expedition in California when he

The desert crossing continued to be a story of misery and hardship. The alien landscape was a hard surface of salt and alkali where almost no plants or grasses could survive. Thick clouds of alkali dust swirled around the party constantly, raised by the animals' hooves, the wagons' wheels, and the pioneers' footwear.

received orders from President James K. Polk and Secretary of State James Buchanan to arrange with the U.S. envoy to Monterey, Thomas O. Larkin, for a local rebellion against the Mexican government. Frémont's secret orders suggested "that American rifles in California might be handy in case trouble with Mexico came to a head."[*] To an extent, the fact that so many *Californio* landowners, including Colonel Mariano Vallejo, were dissatisfied with Mexican rule simply helped Frémont in his revolutionary efforts.

By July 7, 1846, the U.S. Navy occupied Monterey and claimed possession of Northern California. In a short matter of days, "the Stars and Stripes were also flying over Yerba Buena [today's San Francisco], New Helvetia [Sutter's Fort], and (replacing the short-lived Bear Flag) Sonoma."[**] Frémont and U.S. Marine Lieutenant Archibald Gillespie then organized the California Volunteers and marched to Monterey to add to the conquest of California.

Even after establishing the California Bear Flag Republic, Frémont's Bear Flag Revolt had already lost its purpose by becoming part of the Mexican-American War, which resulted in the U.S. acquisition of California. Under the 1848 Treaty of Guadalupe Hidalgo, the Southwest, from California to Texas, became U.S. territory.

Lavender, Great West, *188*.
** *John A. Hawgood*, America's Western Frontiers: The Exploration and Settlement of the Trans-Mississippi West. *New York: Alfred A. Knopf, 1967, 167.*

Sometimes the emigrants could only see a few feet in front of them due to the dust, which burned their eyes constantly. The alkali ravaged their skin. For the oxen, the "salt and alkali were slow poison to them."[12] The water in every spring they reached was brackish and unfit for consumption.

Then, the party reached a rise in the landscape 1,000 feet high. Hope rose with it. Perhaps it signaled the edge of the inhospitable desert. They pushed up the ridge, nearly a full day's effort, but once they reached the summit, their faces fell. Ahead of them lay yet more white, inhospitable, desert moonscape.

Beyond the desert ridge, the ground changed. The dry, alkali flats gave way to sandy dunes "where the animals' hooves and the wheels of the wagons sank inches deep."[13] Here, the Donner Party further fragmented. Emotions had overtaken many much earlier on the trail, and their animosities, jealousies, and self-preservation instincts began to shift into overdrive. Those driving lighter wagons did not intend to remain with their slower-going colleagues. In time, the wagon train stretched a distance of two miles from its advance wagons to its stragglers. With their heavier, overloaded wagons, the Donners and Reeds fell far behind. For the Reeds, the trail was becoming critical. Water was in short supply.

In typical fashion, James Reed mounted his horse and rode hard to the next spring, a distance of 30 miles. Others ahead of him were already unhitching their oxen from their wagons to drive them more quickly to water. When Reed returned to his wagons, he found that his teamsters had allowed 16 of his 18 oxen to wander off into the desert. The Reed wagons were motionless, and with them the Reeds. With death stalking his family, Reed packed them up and walked ahead 10 miles to Jacob Donner's wagon. As Virginia Reed would write, "The family was all asleep, so we children lay down on the ground. A bitter wind swept over the desert, chilling us through and through."[14]

Able to leave his family with the Donners, Reed still had difficult decisions to make. With his oxen scattered, he had to abandon two of his wagons, including the "Pioneer Palace Car." With help from others, he loaded the remaining wagon with essentials only—food, bedding, and clothing. To try and keep American Indians from stealing the contents of the abandoned wagons, they tried to bury them, but struck water just a few inches down. Leaving it all behind, Virginia Reed noted, "when we left the poor old wagon on the [plains], as a monument to past comfort, the looking glass was not even cracked."[15]

Tragedy at Every Turn

Material loss during the desert crossing was not unique to James Reed. George Donner and the Keseberg family each abandoned a wagon as well. Despite such losses in wagons, cargo, and oxen, the desert still lay ahead. Nearly everyone walked to conserve the strength of the remaining oxen and help speed them along. With water in short supply, Tamsen Donner handed out lumps of sugar to her children "moistened with peppermint oil to suck."[1]

The grueling desert crossing did not end until the sixth day, long past the estimate they had been told. The date was September 4, which, according to Hastings's emigrant guide, should have placed the party at the Sierra. With the desert behind them, the party rested for a couple of days while James Reed went in search of his lost oxen. He never managed to find even one, dead or alive. He and a few others returned to his two abandoned wagons and recovered the "palace wagon." Still, he only had two pair of yoked oxen remaining. There would be no sharing among the emigrants regarding the remaining livestock. Reed had to buy another oxen and a cow from a fellow trail member.

TRAIL OF MISERY

They still followed Hastings Cutoff for another two and a half weeks, running south around the Ruby Mountains, then back north. The Donner Party was still following the tracks of Hastings's wagon train. Ironically, four days of travel—including two to the south and two back to the north—brought the party back to within just a few miles of where they had been before. One day's climb over a rolling hill would have landed them at the same location. Days had been lost that could not be recovered. Even the women were cursing the name of Lansford Hastings.

At last, though, the Hastings Cutoff returned to the main trail to California, which the party reached at present-day Elko, Nevada, with the Humboldt River flowing nearby. It was now September 26. So much time had been lost. The wagons from the original party that had remained on the standard trail to Fort Hall and then turned south toward the Humboldt were ahead of them by a month. If they were not already past the Sierra Nevada, they were at least much closer to them than was the Donner Party.

There were few geographic surprises as the party followed the westward flowing Humboldt. They knew to stick to the river until it simply petered out into the Humboldt Sink, where they would enter a much less formidable desert than that through which they had already passed. Then, the Sierra. Despite these certainties of the new trail, the Donner Party had become "so disoriented by their hardships in the desert that they could not be certain of how far they were from Sutter's [Fort]."[2] In fact, they were still 600 miles out, more than seven weeks of travel, even if their oxen managed to keep moving. The party was moving along at a decent clip for the moment, covering an average of 20 miles a day. At night, the larger party split into two different campsites to provide more water and grass for their remaining livestock. Food was becoming critical, so much so that two men—William McCutchen and Charles Stanton—volunteered to ride on ahead to Sutter's Fort beyond the Sierra and pick up supplies. There were also problems with the American Indians in the region, the Diggers, a group of several nations including the Shoshone, Ute, Paiute, Gosiute, Bannock, and others. They were sneaking into the camps at night, stealing horses and oxen. Sometimes they shot livestock with arrows.

Then, during the first week of October, violence of another kind struck the Donner Party. On the fifth, the chain of wagons was moving along a narrow path up a long sand hill, which caused the wagons to squeeze in close together. At one point, one of James Reed's teamsters, Milt Elliott, tried to pass John Snyder, a teamster for the Graves family. The result was that the yokes of oxen on both wagons became enmeshed. Snyder became violently angry and began whipping the oxen, which was not typical behavior for the usually happy-go-lucky teamster. Reed stepped forward to stop Snyder. The young teamster then turned his bullwhip on Reed, hitting him on the head with the whip's handle, causing a deep cut. When Reed's wife, Margaret, ran forward to help her husband, Snyder struck her as well. The wounded Reed then turned on Snyder, pulled out a knife, and stabbed the out-of-control teamster, penetrating his left lung. Snyder died minutes later.

With blood running down his face, Reed was horrified at what had just taken place at his own hand. He staggered to the nearby river and tossed his knife into the water. He and Snyder had never shared a cross word and Reed thought of him as a friend. With Margaret Reed also wounded, she was unable to help her husband. It would fall to Virginia to bandage up

Many American Indians assisted emigrants with finding food, provided medical help, and served as scouts at dangerous crossings. As emigrant numbers multiplied, relations between emigrants and American Indians became strained. Indian life was affected by emigrants who brought disease and killed the wild game. Hostilities and casualties occurred more often after 1860, as seen from the above depiction of an attack on a wagon train.

his wounds. Reed carried scars from Snyder's attack until his death.

Immediately, the men of the Donner Party met to decide how to handle the situation. A murder had been committed within their company. According to some witnesses, Snyder admitted just before he died that he had been in the wrong. This, however, would have no relevance to the decisions that followed. One problem was that the incident had not taken place on U.S. soil, so who had jurisdiction? Another complication was that many members of the party did not like James Reed. Yet another problem was that George Donner, the appointed leader of the party, was not present, with his wagon a full day ahead of the main train. However, he had never applied his leadership during the trek with any authority. When some of the men, including Keseberg, indicated that Reed might be hanged, Reed reacted angrily. As Virginia would describe her father's actions, "he bared his neck, saying 'come on, gentlemen,' but no one moved."[3]

Hanging was not Reed's punishment; his banishment from the party was. Even Reed saw the value of the decision. This would allow him to ride ahead of the main party. At first he was only provided a poor horse and no weapon, but Virginia managed to get him "his rifle, pistols, ammunition, and some food."[4] Reed did ride ahead, reaching the forward wagons in a day. Finding sympathy among that party, he was given more food. He and one of his teamsters, Walter Herron, then moved ahead of the wagon train.

DESCENT INTO NIGHTMARE

The emigrant train, so far behind schedule, so divided by conflicting personalities, and now broken apart by murder, soon descended into absolute tragedy. The Reeds were informed they would have to abandon their "palace wagon," and several others were also told to leave their wagons to help speed the journey. Without James to consult, the Reed family had no choice but to take what clothes and food they had and place them in the Graves family's wagon. The wagons did move faster and finally caught up with the Donners at the front, bringing all the remaining wagons back into a single caravan.

Then, on October 8, just three days after removing Reed from their number, the party lost another member. This time it was from illness. The elderly Hardkoop, nearly 70 years old, had no wagon and had walked the trail until he could do so no longer. Weak from hunger and completely worn out, he could not continue. The party chose to leave him behind. He was never seen again.

Local American Indians kept up their nighttime practice, usually unseen, of shooting occasional arrows into several of the oxen. When the Wolfingers lost oxen, they could not continue with their wagon and so abandoned it. Mr. Wolfinger remained behind to bury his belongings with plans to return some day and recover them. Although the party did not wait for him, two emigrants, Joseph Reinhardt and Augustus Spitzer, went back to help him. After a few days, the two men caught up with the train, claiming Wolfinger had been killed by American Indians. However, some in the wagon party thought the German had been murdered by Reinhardt and Spitzer, assumedly for his wife's jewels or his money belt. At any rate, the Donner Party was down another victim.

Within a week, the party reached Humboldt Sink, the ignoble end of the Humboldt River. The emigrants had been following the river for 12 days. Ahead of them lay another dry stretch of trail, the Forty-Mile Desert. Here, at least, they knew what they were facing; the desert took 24 hours to cross and offered yet more extremes to deal with. One of Patrick Breen's horses fell into a bog at the sink and died even before they set out across the barren desert. The sand shifted under the wagon wheels, sometimes causing them to spin out. Emigrants abandoned nearly everything they did not need.

Just before the party embarked across the desert, a group of Paiute had either stolen or killed William Eddy's remaining livestock, forcing his family to abandon their wagon. By this point on the trail, the party's original 23 wagons had been reduced to 15, and no one seemed willing to share any space with anyone else. Eddy and his wife had no choice but to walk, carrying their two children, an infant and a three-year-old. They had no water or food. When Eddy realized that Patrick

After passing the Humboldt Sink, the trail divided into two routes. No matter which was chosen, travelers would have to endure 40 miles without usable water. If travelers took the Carson route, they would walk toward an area called Ragtown, the site of the last potable water on the Carson River. The Forty-Mile Desert (above) was the deadliest and most dreaded part of the California Trail, and was usually crossed at night to avoid the extreme heat.

Breen had some water left in a cask, he pulled a gun to force him to give his children drinks.

The struggle through the sandy desert ended at a sulfur spring where many washed their clothes and hung them out to dry in the first trees they had seen in some time. The stop became known as Ragtown.

On October 16, the worn out emigrants began their trek along the Truckee River, which led them directly into the Sierra Nevada. The party experienced some joy when Eddy went hunting along the river and returned having bagged nine geese. But between 80 people or so, the birds did not go far. After Paiute killed another ox, the party almost happily slaughtered the animal for food.

REUNION AND DISASTER

The wagon train continued along the Truckee in the shadow of a rocky canyon. After four days along the river, the party was elated by the return of Charles Stanton, who, along with two American Indian guides, was leading seven pack mules carrying flour, meat, and even dried fruit. McCutchen, who had ridden ahead with Stanton, had fallen ill and stayed back at Sutter's Fort. Just as important as the food was the addition of the Miwok guides whom Sutter had sent along to help the Donner Party to the sanctuary of his fort and the great San Francisco Valley. Stanton also informed the party that James Reed and Walter Herron had reached the fort, although Reed's horse had died. The two men had nearly starved, surviving for a week on some beans that had fallen out of one of the wagons with the Hastings Party. Reed was organizing a rescue party, Stanton said.

Amid all the information Stanton gave to the Donner Party, he managed to give some bad advice. Mountain men at the fort had told him that the big snows in the Sierra usually did not come until mid-November. Since the calendar read October 20, he told the party they would make the fort in plenty of time. For that reason, the party decided to stop and rest for a few days. They even put the decision to a vote, and all the adults chose unanimously to stay put and rest. The party had reached the Truckee Meadows, "a pleasant, grass-covered flat near the foot of the Sierras."[5] (Today, Reno, Nevada, occupies the site.) The emigrants had crossed the Truckee River back and forth 22 times.

That night, tragedy again found its way to the Donner Party. While sitting around a campfire, William Pike, one of the Murphy family's son-in-laws, was cleaning his pistol, a pepperbox model. While handing or tossing the handgun to his brother-in-law William Foster, the gun discharged and shot the 25-year-old Pike in the back. He died within an hour, leaving a wife and two baby girls. As the party buried Pike, a light snow began to fall; yet they did not return to the trail until October 25, when Patrick Breen decided he could wait no longer. Breen, after all, had lost fewer oxen to American Indian attack or fatigue than anyone else in the party, and he did not want to push his luck any further. As the day went on, others joined Breen. The last to return to the trail were the Donners.

Beyond the meadows, the trail headed toward the sky. Within a day's journey, it entered the forbidding mountain range, becoming steeper with each mile. The emigrants made another river crossing, their forty-ninth in 80 miles, and then the trail took a right turn away from the Truckee River and toward the mountains. This was followed by a left or southern turn that followed the primary Sierra ridge in front of them. More creeks had to be forded. Then, the trail led to a mountain lake, its waters draining into the Truckee below. At the western end of that lake stood the summit ridge of the mountains and the pass the Donner Party had been desperately in need of reaching to avoid the winter snows. From the Truckee Meadows to Truckee Lake (its name would change to Donner Lake in later years), the wagon train had to cover about 50 miles.

Just getting their wagons up the eastern face of the Sierra was a nightmarish ascent, filled with high cliffs, great granite boulders wedged loose from the cliffs by frost, and sudden drop-offs. Scrub made the going more difficult and concealed many pitfalls. The wagon trail wound a tentative way among these dangers. Tall, grim crags loomed on either side of the pass, which was a narrow opening between some lower rocks. Even in summer there could be bone-chilling winds at the summit almost strong enough to knock a man down.[6]

A strong team of oxen could cover the distance from the meadows to the lake in three days. The fastest any members of the Donner Party managed to do it was twice that time. Others needed additional days. Then, during the first night of the ascent, a lone American Indian shot one arrow each into 19 oxen. Eddy spotted the attacker and shot him, and the man's body fell down a mountain embankment into a thicket of trees. The wounded oxen were hardly able to continue.

A RACE WITH THE WEATHER

As they ascended, snow fell. It soon covered the trail, as well as nearby grasses, which was fodder for the oxen. Up the mountainside, the emigrants saw nothing but a sheet of white. On October 31, the first of the party reached Truckee Lake. Less than a mile away stood an abandoned cabin that had been built by members of the Stevens Party who had opened up the trail through the Sierra just two years earlier. No one chose to stay in the cabin that night.

The following morning, it appeared that heavy snows had fallen ahead in the pass. With clouds lying low, the party got lost in fog and returned to the lake and the cabin, which the Breen family decided to claim. Later in the day, stragglers arrived at the lake, including the Reed family. They reported that the Donners were having serious trouble with their wagons. While cutting a new axle out of a tree, George Donner had cut his hand severely, losing large amounts of blood.

New days brought new problems. On November 2, rain kept them from moving, but some thought the rain would help melt snow on the trail ahead. The following morning the sun came out with a blaze. The emigrants hit the trail. But the previous day's rains had fallen as snow in the pass and "the wagons could not be dragged through the snow," so the pioneers loaded what they could onto their oxen and started again.[7] When snows still held them up, they stopped in their tracks. If they were waiting for ideal circumstances to make their crossing over the pass, they might not proceed at all. Stanton was ahead of the main party and soon returned, reporting, as Virginia Reed would later write, "that we could get across if we kept right on, but that it would be impossible if [more] snow fell."[8]

The discouraged emigrants did not follow Stanton's warning. Instead, they began to light campfires and removed their belongings from the backs of their oxen. Stanton was angry at their response, certain they did not understand they were standing on the edge of personal peril. One of the Miwok pointed into the cloudy, wintry sky, toward the moon, which was encircled with an ominous ring that meant heavy snows. This might be the party's final opportunity to make the Sierra crossing to safety. More snow could soon block their path. But the majority of the party stayed motionless, claiming great fatigue, and was mentally prepared to take up the march over the pass on the following day.

The winds of fate blew in overnight, delivering a foot of new snow across the pass, making the Donner Party's only avenue to safety and survival impassable.

The Taboo

One more day. That is all they needed to stumble through the snowy pass of the Sierra Nevada leading to the safety of Sutter's Fort. But they had waited at the wrong moment on the trail and for too long. Everyone in the party could likely recall a time and place along the trail since leaving Springfield, Illinois, or Independence, Missouri, or Fort Bridger, when the party stopped to rest themselves and their animals. Everyone could probably pick a single day on the trail, perhaps months earlier, when they should have made progress rather than remain motionless.

A CLOSED DOOR

Such regrets were of no use now. The snows had come with a vengeance, caring little for the plight of the emigrant train that had struggled from back East to the wrong side of the mountains. For all practical purposes, "The Sierra Nevada had slammed shut on the Donner Party like a prison door."[1] Perhaps the words of Lansford Hastings's trail guide would haunt the members of the stranded party through the nightmare that lay ahead for them: "Unless you pass over the mountains early in the fall, you are very liable to be detained, by impassable mountains of snow, until the next spring, or, perhaps, forever."[2]

Members of the party did not panic. They soberly assessed their difficult situation and began taking steps to settle in around Truckee Lake. The Breens had claimed the cabin, which was serviceable, even if its walls were made of pine boughs and ox hides. It measured 16 by 20 feet and included a fireplace. The cabin had a dirt floor, and nothing inside except some books abandoned by its previous occupants, including a Bible, a book of Shakespeare, and *The Life of Daniel Boone*. Along one side of the Breen cabin, the Kesebergs built a lean-to. Others began working on cabins of their own. The Reeds, the Graves, and Stanton and his American Indian companions built an extended cabin with two doors, its roof covered with ox hides. The Graves lived in half of the cabin and the others lived in the second half. Yet another cabin was built alongside a large triangular-shaped outcropping of granite at the campsite. This provided shelter for the Murphys, Fosters, Eddys, and Pikes. These four shelters, in close proximity to each other, provided living quarters for about 60 people.

The Donners, however, had not yet reached Truckee Lake. They were stranded back on the trail, about six miles away at Alder Creek. A broken axle had stopped them on the trail. Now the axle would be of no use. They would have to build shelters too. They began to erect three tents, covering them over with logs, brush, India rubber raincoats, and blankets. These makeshift shelters would house the Donners, Mrs. Wolfinger, and the four teamsters, a total of 6 men, 3 women,

At the end of October 1846, the Donner Party became trapped by snow-drifts over 20 feet high in the Sierra Nevada Mountains. Three-quarters of the travelers camped at a lake (now called Donner Lake) in cabins, while the Donner family and a few others camped in tents about six miles away at Alder Creek. This painting shows the Donner Party huddled in a tent in the mountains.

and 12 children. Between those at Alder Creek and Truckee Lake, the Donner Party numbered 81 people.

Along with shelter, the party needed food. Hunting was almost out of the question, for the game had already gone down to the valleys for the winter season, too far away to find now. Eddy did go out and try hunting for a while, bagging a scrawny coyote and an owl. When the party encamped at Truckee Lake, the water was not yet frozen over and large trout could be seen. Fishing parties did try to catch some fish, "but the fish were logy with the cold and would not bite. It never occurred to anyone to make nets to catch the plentiful fish."[3]

DESPERATE CIRCUMSTANCES

Unable to feed their livestock, they then slaughtered the oxen, which provided needed meat and ox-hide coverings to roof the cabins. In most instances, the oxen were cut into quarters and the meat left in the snows where it would be preserved by the cold. Since nearly all cooperation had left the party long ago, the meat for the slaughtered animals was not shared. If a family had oxen, they kept the meat for themselves. Some families were desperate for food almost immediately. The Reeds were particularly in a bind. Bargains were hard driven. Sometimes, selfishness and greed seemed to know no limits. On November 9, when one of Graves's oxen died, he did not think the thin animal worth keeping to feed his own family, but he charged the Eddys $25 for the dead animal.

Virginia Reed recalled the bargain her mother agreed to with others who had oxen: "My mother had no cattle to kill but she made arrangements for some, promising to give two for one in California."[4] When the Irishman Patrick Dolan offered meat to Margaret Reed, he demanded payment in the form of James Reed's pocket watch and Mason's medal. The Reeds had five dogs earlier on the trail, but had lost four along the way. They would wait a while before they decided to kill Cash, the remaining terrier, for food.

The first weeks at Alder Creek and Truckee Lake were spent establishing shelter and preparing food stores. For some, however, food was in such short supply that to simply remain in camps would mean certain starvation. By mid-December, 15 members of the party, 10 men and 5 women, decided to try and scale the snow-packed mountain pass in front of them. Franklin Graves fashioned crude snowshoes for the group that would become known as "Forlorn Hope." The party included Patrick Dolan, Franklin and Mary Graves, Charles Stanton, William Eddy, and the two American Indian guides, Luis and Salvador. Virginia Reed had planned to go with them, but she became sick and had to drop out. As the "snowshoers" headed up toward the pass, the Donner Party members left behind could have some hope. They also held out hope for the rescue reportedly being mounted by James Reed on the other side of the pass. (At the time, the Donner Party could not have known that James Reed was already floundering in his efforts to get back to them; the deep snows were stopping him and William McCutchen in their tracks.) On the same day the snowshoers headed out of camp, the Donner Party suffered another casualty: 24-four-year-old Baylis Williams, "crazy with fever, cries out and dies."[5]

Back down at Alder Creek, the Donners were suffering incredibly. George Donner's hand had become infected from his earlier accident. They had only been able to erect tents, having almost no strength to build log cabins, and so they were constantly cold. Their clothes and shoes were wet since there was no way to keep anything dry. Basically, only thin quilts and canvas protected them from the elements. Faced with these circumstances, death soon reached the Donner encampment. By late December, three of the Donners' teamsters had died, as well as Jacob Donner.

"THE SNOWSHOERS" SET OUT

With the snowshoers on their way, those left behind focused on the things that meant the difference between death and survival. Days passed and Christmas arrived, but celebrating was not to be the order of the day—except, perhaps, for the Reed children. Margaret Reed produced the makings for, under the circumstances, a Christmas feast. She had earlier squirreled away a piece of bacon, no bigger than a child's hand, which she now produced, along with a small amount of beans and rice, and some dried apples. It was food that the Reed family would otherwise have taken for granted. Joining the Reeds in their dinner were Milt Elliott, who had stayed by the family through their difficulties, as well as the family maid, Eliza Williams, whose brother, Baylis, had recently died. As Margaret served her extended family their Christmas meal, she said something she would not repeat any time soon: "Eat slowly, for this one day you can have all you wish."[6]

For nearly everyone stranded at the lake or Alder Creek, the usual fare was a soup boiled down from ox hides. Typically, a hide was first cut into strips. Once the hair was singed off, the hide was boiled for several hours, and then cooled. The result was a gooey mixture that nearly everyone hated, except, it appears, for the Breen family. As bad as this tasted, there were worse foods. The Murphy family actually consumed a rug that had been originally fashioned out of animal skin. With the rug close to the Murphy fire, the children figured out they could break off small chunks and roast them. Everything became fodder for a meal. The leather from shoes and books was boiled into gruel. The Reeds finally broke down by the New Year and killed the family dog, Cash. The meat from the terrier lasted the family for a week. No part of the dog was wasted. As Virginia would write, "We ate his entrails and feet & hide & evry thing about him."[7]

For the Reeds, their dog was the last of their food, which drove Margaret Reed to make a desperate decision. She would try and scale the pass with Milt Elliott, Eliza Williams, and her eldest, Virginia. Somewhere on the other side, she wanted to believe, she would find her banished husband. This party set out on January 4, a warm morning. Margaret's remaining children—Patty, James, and Thomas—were sent to stay with the Breen and Graves families. When the younger children balked at their mother's leaving, she told them, "we would bring them Bread & then thay was willing to stay."[8]

After only a few days, however, the desperate party returned to the encampment by Truckee Lake. The pass was blocked by snow, and Margaret's compass had broken. It was just as well they gave up, for that very night "thare was the worst storme we had that winter & if we had not come back that night we would never got back," wrote Virginia.[9]

DEATH IN THE CAMPS

By late January, death had visited the encampments repeatedly. On January 4, one-year-old Margaret Eddy died, with her mother, Eleanor, joining her three days later. Only three-year-old James Eddy was left, still in the care of Mrs. Murphy, who was slowly becoming delirious, blinded by starvation. On the last day of that month, John Landrum Murphy, age 15, died. Two days later, the McCutchen baby, Harriet, who was in the care of Mrs. Graves, died. August Spitzer died in the early morning hours of February 8, after asking Mrs. Breen for some meat, but receiving nothing.

During the weeks following their aborted attempt to leave the camp and scale the pass, the Reeds faced new difficulties. Forced to boil some of the ox hides that had served as roof material for their cabin, the Reeds were soon confronted by the Graves, who said the hides belonged to them. It was Elizabeth Graves who made the greater fuss about the disputed ox hides. As Breen would describe her: "She is a case."[10]

Fortunately for the Reed family, the Breens offered to share their cabin with them. For Virginia, the Breens were, literally, a lifesaver. Virginia had returned with her feet seriously frostbitten, and Mrs. Breen provided her with small amounts of food. For everyone, food shortages and death walked hand in hand. As the younger John Breen would later write: "Death had become so common an event that it was looked upon as a matter of course, and we all expected to go soon."[11] In fact, just weeks following the failed attempt to scale the pass, Milt Elliott died from a lack of food. Virginia Reed helped bury him and later wrote, "Poor Milt! it was hard to cover that face from sight forever, for with his death our best friend was gone."[12]

The world of those encamped on the wrong side of Truckee Pass became a twilight existence. When the snow-drifts outside were too high to maneuver around in, people were obliged to cut off pieces of their shelters to feed their fires. No one had any energy, and hard work was impossible. Even sitting was difficult, for the emigrants were losing the body fat that normally padded their backsides. People lay about, trying to stay warm, unable to even move on some days. Some turned to their faith to sustain them through these difficult struggles. The Breen cabin was opened to those who wanted to come and read from the Bible, sing, and pray. Believers fell to their knees, asking for God's mercy. Hunger brought on hallucinations as Patty Reed claimed to see visions of angels, as well as devils. Virginia wrote, "I never think of that cabin but that I can see us all of the ground, praying. I can see my Mother planning and wondering what else she could do for her children."[13]

February brought another visitation, this time from a human being from the outside. Patrick Breen would write about the visitor who could not communicate with the suffering emigrants:

> One evening, as I was gazing around, I saw an Indian coming from the mountain. He came to the cabin and said something which we could not understand. He had a small pack on his back, consisting of a fur blanket, and about two dozen of what is called California soaproot . . . He appeared very friendly, gave us two or three of the roots, and went on his way.[14]

The emigrants ate the soaproot, which had a flavor reminiscent of sweet potatoes.

There was in fact a group of American Indians watching the stranded pioneers. As Sarah Winnemuca, the granddaughter of Chief Truckee, would write four decades later: "Those were the last white men that came along that fall . . . white people perished in the mountains, for it was too late to cross them. We could have saved them, only my people were afraid of them. They must have suffered fearfully . . . the snow was too deep."[15]

A handful of soaproot could not save the emigrants, and food was almost impossible to find by the early part of 1847. The gnawing hunger felt by nearly all would finally drive some among the Donner Party to suggest the unthinkable: With those among their number dying with regularity, could not their bodies be consumed for food?

THE UNSPOKEN

The party of snowshoers had actually been the ones to first suggest cannibalism. The party was met with disaster piled on top of disaster just as the snows piled endlessly on one another. When they left the Truckee Lake encampment, they estimated it would take them six days, traveling five miles a day, to reach the first white settlement on the other side of the pass. They carried rations for only those days, which were thin anyway, along with a blanket apiece and no other clothing. Their trek took much longer than expected.

They suffered at every miscalculated step. New snows fell, nearly burying them. By day, they suffered from snow blindness, and they could barely see to keep going. Their snowshoes fell apart. By day seven, they were out of food, and too many miles from rescue. Then, Charles Stanton died. That Stanton had returned after making it to Sutter's Fort in order to help the Donner Party in its plight was a selfless act. He had no family among those he had left behind, and he could

Feeling a sense of desperation, 15 members of the trapped party, later known as Forlorn Hope, set out on crudely made showshoes for Sutter's Fort, about 100 miles away. This group of 10 men and 5 women soon ran out of food and were caught in a snowstorm without shelter. Starting out in mid-December 1846, they finally reached their destination on January 18, 1847, with two men and five women.

easily have washed his hands of the whole mess once he had climbed beyond the pass into the Sacramento Valley. But he had chosen to go back, having promised the same. Now, he was dead, having succumbed to a lack of food. The Donner Party would miss his leadership and example.

As Stanton died, no one spoke of consuming his body. Fortunately, William Eddy discovered a half-pound of bear meat in his pack, hidden away by his wife, along with a well-wishing note from "your own dear Eleanor."[16] Eddy shared the find with his fellow snowshoers, which staved off their own deaths for a handful of days.

Then, Patrick Dolan finally brought up the subject that no one wanted to discuss. The thought of cannibalism sickened them all. Mary Ann Graves wrote: "Even the wind seemed to hold its breath as the suggestion was made that were one to die, the rest might live."[17] Someone suggested that they draw names for a victim. Eddy proposed two of them have a shoot-out. In the end, they decided to wait until someone died a natural death. They did not have long to wait.

That very night, their campfire melted too much snow and the fire was extinguished. A panic ensued, leading Patrick Dolan to hallucinate from hunger. Before the night was over, Dolan died, along with three others—Antonio the teamster, teenager Lem Murphy, and Franklin Graves. It was ironic that the first person to be cannibalized was Dolan, the very one who had made the macabre proposal the previous day. It was the day after Christmas that his companions made a fire and began hacking off pieces of Dolan's flesh from his limbs. Perhaps with shame, the desperate party members "roasted the lean, stringy meat over the campfire and ate it, turning their faces away from each other."[18] Three members of the party could not make themselves participate—William Eddy, and the two American Indians, Luis and Salvador.

Despite their initial hesitance, though, the members of the snowshoeing party who had engaged in cannibalism began to accept the practice without much restraint. They harvested their former comrades' hearts, livers, and brains. They dried much of the remaining flesh to eat later. After eating and resting for three days, they were ready to return to the trail. The group did take one thing into consideration as they ate human flesh: It was decided that no one should consume any meat from a relative. Pains were taken to identify each piece of "meat" by name. In all, they consumed their cannibalized party members for a week. Then, they were again without anything to eat.

The conscience of William Foster allowed him not only to eat human flesh; he then suggested that the two American

Indians be killed for food. William Eddy stopped him, reminding Foster that the group had decided not to kill anyone for food. To further thwart Foster's cold-blooded plans, Eddy warned Luis and Salvador, who quickly abandoned the group and ran off. Fortunately, Eddy was able to kill a deer that lasted the party a few days. Then, they discovered Luis and Salvador on the trail, dying from starvation. Foster finally had his way and killed the two men, who did not have the strength to resist him. Only Foster and the pair of women in his family ate this flesh. Everyone else chose to refrain.

THE MEXICAN-AMERICAN WAR

As the Donner Party struggled along Hastings Cutoff, the Mexican-American War was in full swing. Its outcome would determine the future of California, where the party of emigrants was heading.

At the opening of the war in the spring of 1846, President Polk sent General Zachary Taylor south, along the Rio Grande, deeper into Mexican territory. In addition, the president sent Colonel Stephen Kearney into New Mexico and California, where U.S. troops were to occupy northern Mexican cities, such as Palo Alto and Monterrey. U.S. forces captured both towns in May and September, respectively.

Following a march of 900 miles, Colonel Kearney arrived in Santa Fe, New Mexico, where nearly the entire local population surrendered peacefully. He then marched on to California where he took control with the help of U.S. naval forces and a handful of tenacious revolutionaries living in California, which were led by army explorer John C. Frémont.

The group slogged on with cannibalism and murder now a part of their legacy. They reached an American Indian village where they were fed pinon nuts and a bread made from acorns. The American Indians then led William Eddy to a group of emigrants who had managed to get over Truckee Pass, but had been stranded on the west side of the mountains. They were encamped at Bear Valley, 40 miles from Sutter's Fort. The men in the party backtracked Eddy's path, which included bloody footprints left by his frostbitten feet, to the other snowshoers struggling 6 miles behind.

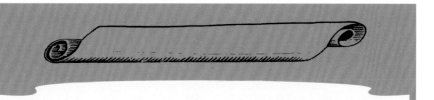

With U.S. victories in both California and New Mexico, Polk anticipated that the Mexican government would be prepared to sue for peace and write terms of surrender. But the Mexicans did no such thing. This forced Polk to dispatch General Taylor southward. In February 1847, Taylor engaged Mexican troops under the command of General Santa Anna at Buena Vista, near Monterrey, Mexico (not to be confused with Monterey, California). Santa Anna was unable to defeat the hard-driven U.S. commander. Within weeks, more U.S. forces, under the command of General Winfield Scott, landed U.S. troops in the Mexican city of Veracruz, along the Gulf Coast.

General Scott continued his march across Mexico, toward the capital, Mexico City. U.S. casualties ran high as Scott's troops moved further into the Mexican interior. Their advance was slow, requiring six months of hard fighting, as U.S. forces faced a constant, daily challenge from Mexican guerrillas. But by September 1847, Scott's forces arrived in the Mexican capital and occupied the city, effectively ending the military action of the war.

At last they were relatively safe. Their 6-day trek had extended to 33 days. It was mid-January. Of the 15 snowshoers, 8 were dead, all males. Only William Eddy and William Foster were still alive, along with all of the women. Eddy soon wrote a letter and had it delivered to Sutter's Fort. In it he described the circumstances of the Donner Party: They had not made it over the pass in time, and their situation was desperate.

"Do You Come from Heaven?"

Two rescue parties were organized, one led by James Reed. The other was led by Aquilla Glover, a friend of the Donners and Reeds, and a fellow Illinoisan who had immigrated to California the previous year. Just organizing such a party proved difficult due to other events taking place in California at the time. The United States's war with Mexico meant that many of the able-bodied men in the Sacramento Valley had gone off to fight. Reed himself had volunteered and engaged in the Battle of Santa Clara in early January.

He decided to travel to Yerba Buena (modern-day San Francisco) in an attempt to raise recruits for a rescue party, but he only managed to enlist a few sailors there. Then the war ended, at least in California, on January 10, with the capture of Los Angeles by U.S. Marines. By the end of the month, Glover's party of rescuers, including 10 volunteers, had headed eastward on the trail toward the stranded wagon parties.

"GAUNT WITH FAMINE"

The rescue party faced its own share of difficulties carrying out its mission of mercy. Some of the men in the party were paid $3 a day—a good wage at the time—but nevertheless three of Glover's party quit along the way, turned back by the high snowdrifts. The snowdrifts were 10-feet deep in places and their packhorses balked at both these and at crossing icy creeks. Glover's rescuers took three weeks to reach the Donner Party encampment at Truckee Lake, spotting the emigrant camp on February 18. Reed's group was behind them somewhere.

They arrived late in the day, the sun having descended on the western side of the mountains. As the men entered the camp, they saw no sign of life, "not even a wisp of smoke."[1] The men thought they might have arrived too late. They raised shouts and then, out of the snow, the gaunt figure of a woman emerged from a hole. The stranded emigrants had taken to the practice of burrowing into the snow when the sun was out and warm, since the snow provided insulation. The woman staggered toward them, looking like a ragged scarecrow. "They were gaunt with famine," noted one of the rescuers, "and I can never forget the horrible, ghastly sight they presented."[2] Others rose out of the snow and came toward the men, uncertain whether they were real or a hunger-induced vision. The woman spoke with a hollow voice: "Are you men from California? Or do you come from heaven?"[3]

For the rescuers, they had never seen such a miserable sight. The encampment was filthy with human waste and slaughtered animal bones. No one seemed to have had any sympathy for anyone who was not a part of his or her family. The Californians had not envisioned the full level of desperation, suffering, and near-insanity that seemed to have taken over some of the Donner Party emigrants. Once it became clear that

An archaeologist holds a bone fragment found in the soil at a site near Truckee, California, in 2004. Researchers tested the bone for DNA to determine whether it was human, but results were inconclusive. Archaeologists have also unearthed a cooking hearth, musket balls, jewelry beads, and wagon parts.

the men were real, from California, and with food, the rescue group represented new hope for the starving emigrants. As one of the rescuers, Reason "Dan" Tucker, wrote, we "found the people in great distress such as I have never witnessed, there having been 12 deaths and more expected every hour . . . the sight of us appeared to put life into their emaciated frames."[4]

The rescuers had to be careful not to give the emigrants too much food at once, for they would kill themselves by over-consuming. That night, a guard was placed near the provisions to keep anyone from stealing food that might cause death rather than save them.

The following morning, three of the rescuers went on to the Donner camp with some food. The Donners were down to their last ox hide. Jacob Donner was dead. At 65 years of age, he had not even started the trip in robust health. George was struggling with an infection in his arm from the accident. Tamsen was in good health, considering the circumstances. She was strong enough to leave with the rescuers and make the walk to Sutter's Fort, but she chose to remain with her husband. Elizabeth Donner, Tamsen's sister-in-law, also chose to stay. One of the family's teamsters, Jean Baptiste Trubode, was prepared to leave with the newly arrived Californians, but they insisted he remain with the Donners. He was the only able-bodied adult male left in the camp.

Six members of the Donner encampment were taken by the rescuers to make the trek on to Sutter's Fort, including four of the older Donner children—Elitha, Leanna, Billy Hook, and George Donner II—plus Mrs. Wolfinger and teamster Noah James.

Before the First Rescue Party had reached the stranded Donners, eight of them had died waiting for someone to return and rescue them. These included four men, a woman, 15-year-old John Murphy, and a pair of infants.

THE RESCUE BEGINS

The rescue party returned to the trail headed west on February 22. Along with six members of the Donner encampment, they took with them the Reed family of five, along with their hired girl, Eliza Williams. The Reeds had run out of food a week earlier and had been living on bones discarded by Mrs. Breen. The two oldest Breen boys, John and Edward, were taken. There were also the two Graves girls and their brother, Billy. Others included an English gunsmith named John Denton, Mrs. Keseberg and daughters Ada and Mary, and son William Murphy, and three-year-old Naomi Pike, who would be carried in a sling by one of the rescuers. (One-year-old Catherine Pike died on February 20, two days after the rescuers arrived

In this photo taken three years after the disaster in the Sierra Nevada Mountains, Mary Murphy (center) holds her infant daughter, Mary Ellen. Her niece Naomi Pike, who was three years old at the time of the ill-fated journey, stands to her left.

at the encampment.) Mr. Keseberg could not go due to a foot injury. In all, the rescuers took 6 adults and 17 children away from the squalor, desperation, and hopelessness of the two Donner Party encampments.

When members of the Donner Party asked about the fate of the snowshoers, the rescuers would only tell them that they had been dramatically slowed down by frostbite. Glover and his men did not want anyone to know, especially those they were leaving behind for later rescue, that more than half the party had perished, and that the other half had survived by cannibalizing the dead. They also did not want them to know that the trek had taken them 33 days rather than the planned 6 days. Such information might only have discouraged those left behind, causing them to give up and die.

To keep these refugees alive and strong enough to travel, the rescuers provided them, through ingenious planning, with an ounce of beef and a small amount of flour twice daily. While they may have left death behind at the encampments, there were no assurances they would all survive the walk to California and civilization.

Everyone had to walk except the youngest two, Naomi Pike and Ada Keseberg, but two of the Reed children, Tommy and Patty, could not keep up. Poor Tommy repeatedly sank into the footprints left by the adults. Glover told Margaret Reed that the two children would have to go back. Even when Glover promised her he would return for them after he had led the rest of the party to Bear Valley, Margaret was uncertain. Only when she learned he was a Mason and that he swore a Mason's oath, would she finally agree. The decision was heartbreaking. As Patty began her walk back to the dark world of the Truckee encampment, she turned to her mother and said, "Well, Ma, if you never see me again, do the best you can."[5]

NEW NIGHTMARES

Within four days of the departure of the First Relief Party, those left behind at Truckee Lake mentioned cannibalism for the first time, as recorded on February 26 by Patrick Breen in his diary: "Mrs. Murphy said here yesterday that [she] thought she would commence to Milt and eat him. I don't think that she has done so yet, it is distressing."[6]

With the Reed family gone, no one could protect the frozen body of their young male friend lying in a snow bank. Indeed, Milt's two-weeks-dead body was soon dragged from a drift and Lavina Murphy cut out his heart and liver to prepare for consumption. Whatever twinge of conscience Murphy may have had, she could not know that the snowshoers had already done the same two months earlier. She and the others at Truckee Lake were also not aware that the Donners at Alder Creek were already consuming the bodies of Jacob Donner and teamster Samuel Shoemaker. At both Alder Creek and Truckee Lake, those who ate human flesh followed the same rule set by the snowshoers: Relatives were careful not to eat the flesh of kin.

In the mountains, the rescue party and the rescued struggled along. The youngest children, including five-year-old Jimmy Reed, floundered with each step. So small, "he would have to place his knee on the hill of snow between each step of the snowshoes and climb over; he was too small to reach from one step to the other."[7] To urge the poor boy on, the rescuers told him his father would buy him a pony if he made it to California and that he would never have to walk anywhere again. Margaret and Virginia Reed became extremely concerned for little Jimmy, and for good reason. On February 24, three-year-old Ada Keseberg died, and her thin body was buried in the snow.

Fortunately, Tommy continued his progress and made it through the pass after six days of climbing. There were still many obstacles ahead, including more snow and difficult mountain trails, but the young boy was soon buoyed when they crossed paths with James Reed and the Second Rescue Party. Reed had been away from his family for four months. The reunion was recorded by one of the Reed children: "My mother dropped on the snow. I started to run to meet him, kept falling down, but finally was folded in my dear Father's arms once more. 'Your mother, my child, where is she?' I pointed towards her, I could not speak."[8] Despite being reunited with his family, Reed was stunned by the appearance of those who had struggled to survive for months on the wrong side of Truckee Pass. As he later wrote, "I can not describe the death-like look they all had. Bread Bread Bread was the begging of every child and grown person except my Wife."[9] Also among this Second Rescue Party was William McCutchen, who sadly learned of the death of his one-year-old child.

Almost as soon as James Reed was reunited with most of his family, he left them to continue on, realizing that Patty and Tommy were still awaiting rescue, having been unable to continue with the First Rescue Party. He was afraid they might die before he could get to them. As for the first party and their rescued, they continued on down the mountain to Johnson's Ranch. Virginia was happy to finally be in California: "No more dragging over the snow, when we were tired, so very tired, but green grass, horses to ride, and plenty to eat."[10] For one of the rescued, too much food led to his death. Soon after reaching the ranch, 12-year-old William Hook, one of Jacob Donner's stepsons, overate and died, his strained body unable to adjust from famine to feast.

THE SECOND RELIEF PARTY ARRIVES

The First Rescue Party reached Johnson's Ranch on February 28. The next day, James Reed and his party of nine rescuers reached Truckee Lake. Patty was sitting in the sun on top of a cabin and saw them coming. As she ran to her father, she fell from weakness. Reed asked her about Tommy. He was in a snow hole to stay warm, Patty explained. Reed soon found him, so thin and weak. At first, young Tommy did not even recognize his father, asking Patty who "that man" was.[11] Bread was the second miracle of the day, as James Reed handed a little to both of his starving children.

Above is a picture of a small wooden doll owned by eight-year-old Patty Reed. Historians say Patty slipped the doll into her apron pocket when her family had to abandon their wagon in the Great Salt Lake desert. "Dolly" was part of a six-month exhibit at the Smithsonian Institution called "1846: Portrait of the Nation" in 1996.

Reed and the rescuers then looked for other survivors. He and McCutchen checked the Murphy cabin and discovered Lavina Murphy there, half blind and half insane. As she tried to speak to her rescuers, she laughed and cried at almost the same moment. They found toddlers Georgie Foster and James Eddy lying on a pallet in their own excrement and thick with lice. The boys begged for food and were soon fed. Reed and McCutchen cleaned the boys up with soap, washed their clothes, oiled their raw skin, and wrapped them up in flannel. Keseberg was in miserable condition and almost immobile. After Reed washed his own children, he washed Keseberg, the very man who had months earlier suggested Reed be hanged. When the humbled Keseberg asked for someone else to clean him up, Reed said "he was willing to let bygones be bygones."[12] The rescuers went from cabin to cabin. It was the same in each: skeletal inhabitants, human waste, filthy clothes, and lice.

Reed and McCutchen found something else that surprised and sickened them. In the dark confines of the Murphy cabin, they came upon the remains of Milt Elliott. Almost his entire body had been consumed, even as his face had gone unmarked. There were other signs of cannibalism: "Half-consumed limbs lay partly hidden in trunks, and human hair of different colors was strewn in tufts around the fireplace. The sight was too much to bear. Reed and McCutchen cried out in grief and horror and burst into tears."[13] There is no record of what the Second Relief Party found in the Graves's cabin, "but that night they slept outdoors in the clean air, away from the filth, the stench, and the bloodsucking vermin of the cabins."[14]

The next morning, Reed took two of his fellow rescuers along to check on the Donner camp at Alder Creek. Through it all, the living conditions at the creek had not been nearly as squalid and desperate as at the lake encampment. In a matter of recent days, however, conditions had deteriorated. The shelters of the George and Jacob Donner families were about 100 yards apart. At George Donner's, wife Tamsen was down to feeding her children on "a thin slab of tallow . . . out of the dried beef that the First Relief [Party] had left them." The children appeared, to Reed, to look "strong and healthy," along with Tamsen Donner.[15] George Donner, however, was dying,

TREACHERY AT TRUCKEE

When the Second Relief Party led by James Reed left the squalid encampments, they left three of their members behind to watch over the remaining emigrants until the third group of rescuers arrived. But two of the rescuers left behind, Charles Cady and Charles Stone, did not stay at their posts. In fact, they not only abandoned their charges, they also deceived Tamsen Donner into paying them $500 for a task they would not complete.

Cady and Stone had originally been assigned to stay at Truckee Lake. After Reed's rescuers and the rescued left, however, they went down to Alder Creek, where their friend Nicholas Clark had been left. When they arrived, Clark was out following bear tracks he had spotted in the snow. As the two young men talked with Tamsen Donner, a snowstorm seemed to be blowing in. Fearing the Third Relief Party might not be able to get to them due to the storm, she offered to pay Cady and Stone $500 to take her three girls to Sutter's Fort. The men agreed. After taking the girls to say good-bye to George Donner, she combed their hair and dressed them in cloaks and hoods. She then told Eliza, Georgia, and Frances, ages three, four, and six, "I may never see you again, but God will take care of you."*

Tamsen's payment of $500 was extremely generous, yet the two men did not stick to their task for long. When the girls tired and had to be carried, Cady and Stone conferred between themselves and decided to take them back, but not to their mother. They dropped them off at the Murphy cabin, where they were not entirely welcome. The feared storm did roll in and Cady and Stone had to spend the night at the abandoned Breen cabin. They hit the trail the following morning, catching up with Reed and the others in another day or two.

(continues)

Tamsen Donner was unaware that the two young men had deceived her. She was concerned, though, that her daughters might have perished in the snowstorm with Cady and Stone. A week and a half passed before she paid a call at the Murphy cabin. There she discovered her three daughters alive, if not terrorized by the crazed Keseberg. Soon after the girls' arrival, Keseberg had asked to take three-year-old Eliza to his bed. Wary Frances and Georgia refused to let him, so he took Georgie Foster instead. Foster was dead the next morning. Keseberg hung the boy on the cabin wall in front of the girls, and then proceeded to prepare his flesh to eat.

Reunited, Tamsen Donner and her children were safe—at least for the time being.

Limburg, 176.

his infection having spread up the length of his arm clear to the shoulder.

In the Jacob Donner encampment, conditions were much more miserable and horrifying. The rescuers found Jean-Baptiste Trubode carrying a leg from Jacob Donner's body. Trubode explained that the wounded and suffering George Donner had dispatched him after the limb. He said he had received it from Jacob's wife, Elizabeth, who had told him she could not spare another piece of her husband. When Reed and his associates entered Jacob Donner's tent, they found "Jake's children were sitting on a log, their faces messy with blood, eating the half-roasted heart and liver of their father."[16] The children were so detached from any other reality but the food in front of them that they did not even notice the strangers. Reed spoke with Elizabeth Donner, who explained that her family had consumed four of the dead and that her husband's body was the last of their food. A distance away, Reed found the remains of Jacob Donner and others:

> His head had been cut off and was lying face up; the cold had preserved his features unaltered. But his arms and legs had been cut off and his body cut open to remove the nutritious heart and liver. On top of the mutilated corpse lay a leg—Jean-Baptiste had tossed it back when he saw the rescuers coming with more acceptable food. There were other open graves, too, but there was nothing left in them but a few fragments.[17]

Within two days of its arrival, the Second Relief Party was ready to return to California with nearly everyone capable of traveling. This included the Breens, the Graves family, Jacob and Elizabeth Donner's three older children, and Reed's Tommy and Patty. The only people remaining behind at Truckee Lake were Lewis Keseberg, who was crippled; the half-deranged Lavina Murphy and her son, Simon; and the toddlers Georgie Foster and James Eddy. At Alder Creek, Tamsen Donner, plenty healthy to make the trek, refused to abandon her husband. She stayed behind with her three small girls, along with Jean-Baptiste Trubode. Also remaining behind were Elizabeth Donner and her two children, Samuel and Lewis. The two boys were in no shape to travel. Some members of the Second Relief Party remained behind, too; Charles Cady and Nicholas Clark were left at Truckee, and Charles Stone was assigned to the Alder Creek encampment.

They set out on March 3, with those left behind assured that the Third Relief Party would arrive soon.

Nightmare's End

The trek out was miserable and the weather was anything but cooperative. Patrick Breen tried to cheer everyone by playing Jay Fosdick's fiddle. (Fosdick had died with the snowshoers.) Just two days out, a blizzard hit, making even lighting a fire nearly impossible. When fires were lit, several of the emigrants burned themselves by huddling too closely to the flames, their bodies so cold that they could not feel themselves literally on fire. Young Isaac Donner died on March 7 and five-year-old Franklin Graves Jr. passed the following day. The Breen and Graves families felt too weak to continue and chose to wait on the trail for the Third Relief Party. Mary Donner also had to stay with the Breen family of nine, having burned her foot on a campfire.

Reed and the others cut enough firewood to last several days, but could leave no food for the two families. The Breen family was not too worried about the lack of food, though. Mary Breen had a hidden stash of seeds, tea, and sugar.

YOUTHFUL INSPIRATION

Leaving the others, Reed, McCutchen, and their fellow rescuers—Brit Greenwood and Hiram Miller—continued on with Patty and Tommy Reed and Solomon Hook, one of the Donner stepsons. Reed had already sent three members of the rescue party ahead to make certain that the food caches the rescuers had left along the trail were still intact. Miller carried three-year-old Tommy, but eight-year-old Patty stalwartly walked, following in her father's boot prints in the snow. Weak from hunger and freezing, Patty began to hallucinate, claiming to see stars and angels. James Reed and the other men grabbed her up, wrapped her in a blanket, and began to rub her extremities.

James Reed then produced a handful of crumbs he had been saving in the thumb of one of his gloves. Wetting them with his own saliva, he fed them to Patty as if feeding a bird. Thankfully, she recovered, but not enough to walk. Her father carried her in the blanket on his back. As the party trudged on through the cold and snow, even some of the men expressed concerns that they might not make it back to safety at Johnson's Ranch. Young Patty assured them: "No! No! God has not brought us so far to let us perish now!"[1] Her words led some to tears, including McCutchen, who had only recently been informed of the death of his one-year-old child. He declared aloud: "Boys, if there is an angel on earth, Patty is that angel!"[2]

Soon, the Reed rescue party was surprised when two figures appeared from the trail behind them. They were Charles Cady and Charles Stone, whom Reed had left behind to help the Donner Party members left at the encampments. Reed was probably furious with them, but did not do or say anything to them. Only later would he and the others discover the act of betrayal and thievery the two men had done to Tamsen

Donner. For the moment, the two young men were a welcome sight to the tired Reed and McCutchen.

Reed and his party continued down the western slopes of the mountains, their feet cracked and bleeding in the snow. Fortunately, they stumbled upon a cache of food left for them by those Reed had sent ahead; animals had raided several of the other caches. With the needed food in their bellies, they dragged themselves down into Bear Valley and sanctuary at Johnson's Ranch. In a short matter of days, the Reed family was finally reunited at Sutter's Fort, all six safe.

THE THIRD RESCUE

William Foster and William Eddy had been the only two men to survive the snowshoeing party. They had remained at Johnson's Ranch following their harrowing experiences during their month-long trek across the Sierra that had ended in cannibalism and murder. After the return of the First Relief Party, Eddy was informed of the deaths of his wife and infant daughter. He was determined to return to save his three-year-old son, James, who he hoped was still alive. Then, a great storm pushed through the mountains, causing delays in the progress of the Third Relief Party. Finally, on March 7, Eddy and Foster grew impatient and took horses at Johnson's Ranch that the U.S. Navy had provided for the relief effort. Snow or no snow, the two men intended to push their way through the storm to the Truckee Lake encampment.

Along the way, Eddy and Foster caught up with Selim E. Woodworth of the U.S. Navy. A month earlier, Reed had spoken to a meeting in Yerba Buena, California, to raise a rescue party. One of those who volunteered was Woodworth, but he and his fellow volunteers moved slowly, even though the U.S. Navy backed their efforts by providing funds for supplies for the relief mission. Woodworth was moving with four other volunteers and three mules burdened with 400 pounds of flour, as well as other supplies. On March 9, Woodworth's party, along

William Foster was part of the Forlorn Hope Party that traveled 100 miles in an effort to get help. He was one of two men that made it to Sutter's Fort. He and William Eddy organized a Third Relief Party and went back for the others he left behind.

with Eddy and Foster, started out together. Woodworth made it clear he would not attempt to cross the pass, but would establish a supply camp on the west side of the mountains. Eddy and Foster then offered the men $50 each to continue with them to Truckee Lake, but no one accepted their offer.

At that moment, Reed's Second Relief Party reached the Woodworth group. Reed talked Eddy and Foster out of making the trip on their own, and both parties went back down the mountain to try and find other volunteers. Hiram Miller, who had just returned as a member of Reed's Second Relief Party agreed to go back again, only this time he wanted to be paid the $50 Eddy was offering. They then recruited a man named Thompson for another $50. One of Woodworth's party, John Starks, volunteered, as well as a local Mormon named Howard Oakley. Then, Charles Stone volunteered, perhaps feeling guilty about his betrayal of Tamsen Donner and her children. Starks, Oakley, and Stone were to be paid out of Navy funds. The Third Relief Party was assembled.

They set out from Bear Valley on March 11. They made hasty progress and soon reached the dead body of John Denton, still frozen in a seated position. Before he died he had written a poem, the last stanza reading:

> I wish I could once more recall
> That bright and blissful joy,
> And summon to my weary heart
> The feelings of a boy.
> But now on scenes of past delight
> I look and feel no pleasure.
> As misers on their bed of death
> Gaze coldly on their treasure.[3]

HORROR IN THE SNOW

Later that afternoon, the men reached the site where the Breens had refused to continue any farther. There they encountered yet another macabre scene: The campfire had melted down to the earth itself, 25 feet down into the snow, leaving the Breens in a snow pit measuring 12 by 15 feet, "bigger than the cabin where the Breens had spent the winter."[4] There lay Patrick and Peggy Breen, sunning themselves. Around them lay the remains of Mrs. Graves:

> Almost all the flesh had been cut away from her arms and legs. Her breasts were cut off, and her torso had been opened to remove her heart and liver. These were at that moment stewing in a pot over the fire. Beside her sat her little girl, barely over a year old. The child had one arm on the mangled body of her mother, as if to seek comfort, and cried bitterly, "Ma! Ma! Ma!"[5]

Eddy followed a set of steps the Breen boys had cut in the snow and held the child until her cries stopped.

The Breens then explained the events that had taken place over the previous six days. Mrs. Graves had descended into madness and had suggested they kill her baby for food. That night, she died herself, as well as her son Franklin Ward Jr. By day four, according to the Breens, Mary Donner suggested they survive by eating the dead. The boys, Isaac Donner and Franklin Graves, were chosen first, and then Mrs. Graves.

The rescue party conferred and Starks, Oakley, and Stone were selected to take the survivors back to Johnson's Ranch. They left at dawn the next morning and soon reached Bear Valley. For several of the children, John Starks would become one of their favorite memories of their horrible months of nightmare. A large man, weighing nearly 240 pounds, he would carry first one child, then another, sometimes for a mile or two at a time. He was a constant encouragement, laughing with them, and telling them they were no problem for him to carry since they were all such thin children. He promised them they would soon have all the fat meat they could ever want, and good, comfortable sleep. When they reached Bear Valley, there was only a little snow and farther down the mountain, at Mule Springs, no snow at all. As John Breen remembered their arrival 30 years later, "The weather was warm and clear, which gave a sensation to the tired emigrants that I cannot describe."[6]

MORE HORRORS AT TRUCKEE

The four men remaining in the Third Relief Party reached Truckee Lake the same morning that the others arrived at Mule Springs. They went straight to the Murphy cabin where they found Keseberg, who "blandly informed the men that he had eaten their sons."[7] Georgie Foster's grandmother, Lavina Murphy, claimed Keseberg had taken the boy to bed and strangled him, then hung him on the cabin wall before eating the corpse. Keseberg claimed the child had died naturally. He was then asked why he had eaten human flesh when there was a dead ox lying outside in the melting snow. Keseberg "replied matter-of-factly that he preferred human flesh because it tasted better and contained more nourishment."[8] William Foster was enraged. He wanted Keseberg dead, but he could not bring himself to murder the pathetic, demented man. He vowed that, if Keseberg lived and if Foster ever met him again in California under different circumstances, he would kill him.

There were other urgencies besides the ultimate fate of Keseberg. Mrs. Murphy needed rescuing, as well as the three Donner girls. Tamsen Donner, who was already at Truckee, offered Eddy $1,500 to rescue her children, and he said he would do so without receiving any money or else die trying. He also tried to convince Tamsen to come along, too. Eddy and others remembered her as looking fit, even plump, and in good health to make the trek across the mountains. But she would not leave her dying husband, George. She also wanted to get word to Jean-Baptiste Trubode and Clark at Alder Creek, but Eddy told her there was no time, that he could not wait another day, since his food supply was too short. Tamsen then made a fateful decision. She left her three girls in the care of the rescuers—telling them "O, save! Save my children!"[9]—then turned toward Alder Creek and left them without looking back.

The Third Relief Party packed up the three Donner girls and Simon Murphy, Foster's younger brother-in-law, and readied to return to the trail after being in the Truckee encampment for just two hours. As for the demented Mrs. Murphy, they left her in the camp, making her as comfortable as possible before heading out. While still along the lake, the party met up with Trubode and Clark, who had taken off while Tamsen was gone, along with a pack of Donner valuables weighing 40 pounds. The party continued along the pass the next morning, March 14, finding good weather. In a few short days, they reached Mule Springs and were reunited with the survivors of Reed's Second Relief Party. The Donner girls were once again with their cousin Mary. After a few more days, and the girls were taken to Sutter's Fort, where they were joined with their half-sisters, Elitha and Leanna. But their parents, George and Tamsen, remained back at Alder Creek.

THE FINAL ACT

Only a handful of survivors remained on the wrong side of the Sierra. Weeks passed, and then Woodworth received orders to proceed to Truckee Lake with the Fourth Relief Party. Those who volunteered to join him had all participated in earlier relief groups, including Reason Tucker, John Starks, John Rhoads, William Foster, and William Graves.

The party reached Bear Valley only to be turned back by slushy snow and the threat of more snowstorms, perhaps more imagined than real. In fact, most of the men were realistic enough to assume there were probably no survivors left. The crazed Lavina Murphy was surely no longer alive, George Donner's infection must have killed him, and the toddler Sammie had a slim chance of surviving. Tamsen Donner was a regret but, as some reasoned, she had been begged away from Alder Creek twice and refused to go both times. That only left

Leanna Donner was 12 years old when she made the trek west to California with her family. Pictured here as the last survivor of the Donner family, she died June 1, 1930, at the age of 96.

Lewis Keseberg, and no one was interested in risking his own life to save Keseberg's miserable hide.

Not until April 13 did the relief party finally leave Johnson's Ranch. Assuming that those who remained would be dead, one incentive for the members of this party was their legal right to keep, by law, half of any goods they salvaged from the two encampments. The Donners had been wealthy people, and perhaps one more trek over the mountains might finally pay off. Woodworth would not lead the party. Command fell, instead, to a shady figure known as "Captain" William Fallon, a veteran mountain man. Six others joined him, including William Foster. They rode the trail on horseback to Bear Valley, and then set out on foot with 10 days worth of rations. In four days, they were at Truckee Lake. There was little snow on the ground. The Donner Party emigrants had arrived on the west side of the Sierra at the onset of winter, back in early November. The calendar had moved ahead nearly six months. Spring was around the corner, even in the mountains.

With the snow gone, the telltale evidence of human-eating-human was everywhere. The ground was scattered with the remains of human limbs and skulls. The men prepared to search the cabins, certain that no one could possibly be left alive. A sudden shout surprised them. Three American Indians of the Digger group dashed off into the distance, having been surprised by the white men.

Over the next two hours, the relief group searched the cabins for life, but found none. Then they went down to Alder Creek. Amid the scattered remains of books, shoes, and furniture, the Fourth Relief Party found a ghoulish sight. A large iron kettle sat at the doorway of a tent containing pieces of human flesh cut from the body of George Donner. His head lay split open nearby with the brains removed. Next to the kettle, three uneaten ox legs were piled on a chair, all from an ox that had been killed the previous fall, but buried and forgotten in the snow until recently. The meat was still fresh. The men salvaged what few Donner valuables they could find.

A set of tracks led away from Jacob Donner's tent. Three of the party followed them until they disappeared on the bare ground. The men continued in the same direction and

(continues on page 118)

THE DISASTER BY THE NUMBERS

The emigrant wagon train that became known as the Donner Party included 87 emigrants. (This number does not include Sarah Keyes, the mother-in-law of James Reed, who died early, back in Kansas, before the wagon party was named "Donner.") Of that number, 40 did not survive. Among them, 5 died before getting snowed in at Truckee Lake and Alder Creek; 22 died at one of the two winter encampments; and another 13 did not survive their efforts to pass through the mountains, either as part of the snowshoeing party or among the rescued.

Of the families, only two emerged from the nightmare on the trail with no casualties—the six Reeds and the nine Breens. Of all the groups, the one with the greatest death rate was that of individuals with no blood relation to the rest of the Donner Party families. In all, there were 16 such emigrants, all of them male. Some were hired by the Reeds and Donners, and some were single men who attached themselves to the wagon train. Among those 16, all but 3—Jean-Baptiste Trubode, William Herron, and Noah James—did not survive the trek on the trail, the winter on the east side of Truckee Pass, or the rescue attempts. Most of them died before any of the women in the party.

Studies have been done involving the death rates of several other groups within the Donner Party. For example, the death rate among the men was much higher than among the women. Of the males, 30 out of 53, or 57 percent, died, while 10 of 34 women, or 29 percent, died. Statistically, the men died at double the rate of the female members of the Donner Party.

When looking at age and ignoring whether a person was male or female, death rates were highest among the very young and the old. Everyone over the age of 50 died. Most of the children under 5 also died. Children and teens between the ages of 5 and 19 expe-

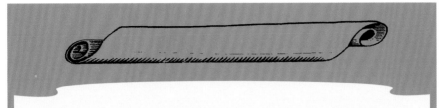

rienced less than a 20 percent death rate, while adults between 20 and 39 experienced a 50 percent rate of death.

Some historians have focused on the dates of death among both males and females, with some interesting results. Of those who died at Truckee Lake or Alder Creek (35 people), 14 men had died by the end of January, but not a single woman. By February, after three months stranded, the women began to die at essentially the same rate as the men. That month saw 11 male deaths and 10 female deaths. What exactly do those two sets of statistics indicate? Some see a clear indication: "Donner Party women were far hardier than the men."[*]

But is such a conclusion accurate? Perhaps the men of the Donner Party were too chivalrous for their own good. Maybe they were practicing the adage of "women and children first." A close study, however, shows this to rarely have been true. Reading emigrant diaries and journals, as well as accounts written later, show "no evidence of hungry men deferring to women, and babies fared especially poorly."[**] Other reasons must be considered. One of these has to do with the level of violence men perpetrated upon other men. Four of the five deaths among Donner Party members that took place before reaching the Sierra, as well as the murders of the two Miwok men, were the result of male-on-male violence.

Another significant consideration lies in the sheer make-up of male and female bodies, in addition to the division of labor between the two sexes, with men more often doing the more physically demanding labor. Since men in general weigh more than women, they need more calories to maintain their basic metabolism. This means the Donner Party men needed more energy than the women, both to do such physical chores as chop wood or hunt, as well as just to maintain their body heat. Even when sitting still, "the typical

(continues)

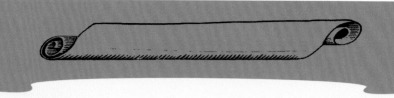

(continued)

metabolic rate for an average-size woman is 25 percent lower than an average-size man's."***

Translation: The men needed a higher intake of calories than the women of the Donner Party, perhaps by as much as 50 percent. But there was simply not enough food to sustain those higher levels in the men. In addition, most women naturally have a higher percentage of body fat than men: 22 percent for women compared to 16 percent for men. Thus, the men of the Donner Party burned up their fat reserves faster than did the women, leading to a higher initial death rate among males.

Jared Diamond, "Living Through the Donner Party," Discover Magazine, March 1992, 105.
** Ibid., 106.
***Ibid., 107.

(continued from page 115)

soon returned to the Truckee Lake cabins. There, they found Keseberg, the last Donner Party survivor, "lying among a disorderly jumble of human bones, calmly smoking a pipe."[10]

Keseberg had not become demented by his circumstances and was unapologetic about his consumption of human flesh:

> Near Keseberg sat two kettles of blood and a large pan full of fresh human liver and lungs. He alleged that his four companions had died natural deaths, but he was frank about having eaten them. As to why he had not eaten ox leg instead, he explained that it was too dry: human liver and lungs tasted better, and human brains made a good soup. As

for Tamsen Donner, Keseberg noted that she tasted the best, being well endowed with fat. In a bundle held by Keseberg the rescuers found silk, jewelry, pistols, and money that had belonged to George Donner.[11]

More than 30 years later, Keseberg was interviewed by a journalist and denied having spoken so favorably of human flesh over ox meat. But "this statement was almost certainly the product of wishful thinking and of the . . . years Keseberg had had in which to . . . regret the dreadful things that had happened in the Sierra snows."[12]

The nightmare of the Donner Party, at least the physical suffering at Alder Creek and Truckee Lake, was finally over. The night of April 23, 1847, was the last that any emigrant of that fateful wagon train would spend trapped on the wrong side of the Sierra Nevada. The following morning, the Fourth Relief Party and Keseberg headed back, arriving at Bear Valley four days later.

Along the way, however, Keseberg experienced one more nightmare. He stopped at a campsite used by an earlier relief party to prepare a pot of coffee for himself. Sitting near his fire, he noticed a piece of clothing sticking out of the snow. With curiosity, he pulled at the cloth and found it to be part of the clothing on a dead body. Ironically, it was Ada, his three-year-old daughter who had perished two months earlier during her rescue by the First Relief Party.

Lives of
the Survivors

Of the 87 members of the Donner Party, 40 did not survive. Of those who did survive, the majority made decent and successful lives for themselves in the land they had struggled so hard to reach. They had gone to California to find new opportunities. Although they had mistimed their trip and miscalculated the perils of the Oregon and California trails, those who survived reached California in time to experience the gold rush of the late 1840s and early 1850s. The United States's war victory over Mexico by 1847 ensured that the Donner Party emigrants would be settling not on foreign land, but on U.S. soil.

SURVIVOR STORIES
Although they had experienced a life-altering ordeal together in the mountains, those circumstances did not encourage the

This statue dedicated to the victims of the Donner Party was built on the site of one of the Donner Party's cabins. The top of the pedestal (about 24 feet above ground) marks the snow depth at this location during the winter of 1846–1847.

Donner Party members to stay in touch with one another. Those who were not related to one another generally lost touch with the other families. In some cases the hatred between certain emigrants was so strong that there was no reason to encourage future contact. History, however, has kept track of many of the survivors.

Their stories are as numerous as the number of survivors. William Foster and his wife, Sarah, settled along California's Yuba River, where they raised a new family. Foster was never tried for the murders of the two Miwok men. William Eddy, the leader of the snowshoeing party, had lost his entire family but settled in California and remarried twice. He never killed Lewis Keseberg for cannibalizing his son, although he did have the opportunity. On one occasion, in San Francisco, Eddy saw Keseberg on a boat in the harbor. He even drew his gun to kill his son's alleged killer, but James Reed, accompanying Eddy, talked him out of it.

Although the parents of the Graves children died, six of the eight children survived. Mary Graves became the first schoolteacher in San Jose. Back East, brother William became a famous lecturer on the Donner Party story. Nancy, who was nine years old during the entrapment in the mountains, suffered psychologically for the rest of her life.

The entire Breen family survived the ordeal and settled down to farm in San Juan Bautista, where they had another child. When gold was discovered, the oldest son, John, became wealthy panning for gold. John and his brother Edward married and had large families, and both were known for their honesty and generosity. The youngest Breen child, Isabella, lived to the age of 90 and was the last survivor of the Donner Party, dying during the Great Depression of the 1930s.

Out of the Murphy family survivors, 13-year-old Mary, with her widowed mother dying in a state of dementia, got married within a week of her arrival in California to one of the owners of Johnson's Ranch. The marriage was a poor one; her husband beat her, and Mary managed to finally receive a divorce. Her second marriage was a happy one. She and her brother William would live as adults in the same California town, Marysville (which her husband named for her), where William was the city attorney.

One of the most tragic figures to emerge from the Donner Party experiences was Lewis Keseberg. Whether he actually murdered Tamsen Donner remains a mystery, but he became a ghoulish symbol of the worst aspects of the whole pioneer party's legacy. He sued for defamation of character those who accused him of murder when he reached California. He won his suit, but the judge only granted him damages of one dollar, a token figure since proving murder was impossible in his case. He and his wife, Philippine, remained together and had eight more children, having lost both their young ones in the mountains. Two of their children were brain-damaged. Nearly all of Keseberg's business ventures ultimately failed, and he eventually withdrew from society.

He may have, at least partially, lost his mind after reaching California. He was quoted many times bragging that he had been a cannibal. Some found Keseberg to be an entertaining oddity for a while, but as the years progressed, he became the object of scorn and criticism. As an older man, young kids would mock him, yelling his name and pelting him with rocks.

Among the Donner families, both sets of parents had died, but eight of the Donner children survived. James and Margaret Reed adopted George's Frances and Jacob's Mary. A Swiss family at Sutter's Fort took in Frances's sisters, Georgia and Eliza. Leanna and Elitha Donner, the two oldest Donner girls, married young and raised the remaining Donner children. All the Donner children lived long lives, with the exception of Mary, who died giving birth to her first child. Eliza Donner's husband would become a U.S. senator from California.

ONE FAMILY'S STORY

The Reed family had survived intact and their collective stories may count as among the most inspiring of the entire ordeal. James and Margaret settled their family in San Jose, south of San Francisco, where James made his fortune in real estate and through the gold rush. As one of the town's founders, he managed to have several streets named for his family, including Margaret, Virginia, Martha, Keyes, and Reed. In San Jose, the Reeds lived in a splendid house and had two more children of their own, plus the two adopted Donner siblings.

Son James Jr. did receive a horse from his father, just as the rescuers had promised him during his trek over the pass. It was said that, as an adult, he rode horses everywhere he went and rarely ever walked. He and his brother Charles became prosperous businessmen like their father. Virginia ran away and got married at age 16 to a young man who had traveled west in the wagon train the Donner Party had followed but never caught up with, the one led by Lansford Hastings. Her husband, John Murphy (no relation to the Donner Party Murphys), became a successful businessman and insurance salesman. They had nine children. Virginia lived to see 87 years of age, and San Jose remained her home for most of her life.

Patty Reed married and also bore nine children. She, too, lived around San Jose. Almost 50 years after the tragic events surrounding the Donner Party, Patty wrote a book about the ordeal, in which she noted: "I sometimes imagine I must be 1,000 years old now, it does not seem to me that I ever was a Child, and yet in many respects I am a Child even now."[1]

Today, the Donner Party legacy is one of uncertainty. Should the pages of U.S. history dote on this single party of pioneers, who lit out for the same West as hundreds of thousands of others did during the 1840s and 1850s, but failed miserably to reach California in a timely manner? Their story is often woven as a morbid tale of deceit at the hands of an emigrant guide author who misrepresented the realities of his infamous cutoff; of constant class clashes between haves and have-nots; of naivety, weak leadership, panic, abandonment, selfishness, murder, depravity, descent into madness, and the consumption of humans by humans. Are these moments to remember?

Indeed, in its most disappointing and lurid circumstances, the Donner Party has become an enduring symbol of miscalculation and moral failure. The mistakes of what may be the most famous wagon train in U.S. history are clear to the modern observer, just as they were to many of their frontier contemporaries. But who among us might have acted differently than they? Living securely in the protective cocoon of the twenty-first century, removed from their primitive world, their circumstantial failures, their animalistic extremes, it is easy for the modern observer to criticize, chastise, and condemn. But who among us can really know how he or she might have chosen to survive through the months at Alder Creek and today's Donner Lake, those seemingly endless days of cold, misery, starvation, and the gnaw of constant hunger? Who among us knows the role he or she might have played, whether that of William Eddy, Tamsen Donner, Lavina Murphy, Elizabeth Graves, Milt Elliott, Patrick Dolan, James Reed, or Lewis Keseberg? Such things may never be known, but the legacy and lessons of the Donner Party must never be forgotten.

LIFE AND DEATH WITHIN THE DONNER PARTY

The Donner Party fell into the annals of U.S. history due to the sensationalism caused by the various acts of cannibalism. In all, the emigrant group that history remembers as "the Donner Party" included a total of 90 members, including 88 emigrants and the two American Indians, Luis and Salvador, who were sent from California as rescuers. This number also includes Sarah Keyes, the Reed children's grandmother, who died early in the trek, back in Kansas. Of those 90 individuals, 47 survived and 43 died. The names are listed below, presented as families, with the exceptions of Mrs. Keyes and the two Miwok men. Also included is the sex of the person, his or her age at the time of the events, and the circumstances and timing of the death of each who did not survive:

DONNER FAMILY

Jacob Donner	M	65	Died in Nov. in winter camp
George Donner	M	62	Died in Apr. in winter camp

(continues)

(continued)

Elizabeth Donner	F	45	Died in Mar. in winter camp
Tamsen Donner	F	45	Died in Apr. in winter camp
Elitha Donner	F	14	
Solomon Hook	M	14	
William Hook	M	12	Died Feb. 28 with 1st rescue team
Lenna Donner	F	12	
George Donner	M	9	
Mary Donner	F	7	
Frances Donner	F	6	
Isaac Donner	M	5	Died Mar. 7 with 2nd rescue team
Georgia Donner	F	4	
Samuel Donner	M	4	Died in Apr. in winter camp
Lewis Donner	M	3	Died Mar. 7 or 8 in winter camp
Eliza Donner	F	3	

MURPHY-FOSTER-PIKE FAMILY

Lavina Murphy	F	50	Died around Mar. 19 in winter camp
William Foster	M	28	
William Pike	M	25	Died Oct. 20 by gunshot
Sara Foster	F	23	
Harriet Pike	F	21	
John L. Murphy	M	15	Died Jan. 31 in winter camp
Mary Murphy	F	13	
Lemuel Murphy	M	12	Died Dec. 27 with snowshoers
William Murphy	M	11	
Simon Murphy	M	10	
Georgie Foster	M	4	Died in early Mar. in winter camp

| Naomi Pike | F | 3 | |
| Catherine Pike | F | 1 | Died Feb. 20 in winter camp |

GRAVES-FOSDICK FAMILY

Franklin Graves	M	57	Died Dec. 24 with snowshoers
Elizabeth Graves	F	47	Died Mar. 8 with 2nd rescue team
Jay Fosdick	M	23	Died Jan. 5 with snowshoers
Sarah Fosdick	F	22	
Mary Graves	F	20	
William Graves	M	18	
Eleanor Graves	F	15	
Lavina Graves	F	13	
Nancy Graves	F	9	
Jonathan Graves	M	7	
Franklin Graves Jr.	M	5	Died Mar. 8 with 2nd rescue team
Elizabeth Graves	F	1	Died soon after rescue by 2nd team

BREEN FAMILY

Patrick Breen	M	40	
Mary Breen	F	40	
John Breen	M	14	
Edward Breen	M	13	
Patrick Breen Jr.	M	11	
Simon Breen	M	9	
Peter Breen	M	7	
James Breen	M	4	
Isabella Breen	F	1	

(continues)

(continued)

REED FAMILY

James Reed	M	46
Margaret Reed	F	32
Virginia Reed	F	12
Patty Reed	F	8
James Reed Jr.	M	5
Thomas Reed	M	3

EDDY FAMILY

William Eddy	M	28	
Eleanor Eddy	F	25	Died Feb. 7 in winter camp
James Eddy	M	3	Died in early Mar. in winter camp
Margaret Eddy	F	1	Died Feb. 4 in winter camp

KESEBERG FAMILY

Lewis Keseberg	M	32	
Philippine Keseberg	F	32	
Ada Keseberg	F	3	Died Feb. 24 with 1st rescue team
Lewis Keseberg Jr.	M	1	Died Jan. 24 in winter camp

MCCUTCHEN FAMILY

William McCutchen	M	30	
Amanda McCutchen	F	24	
Harriet McCutchen	F	1	Died Feb. 2 in winter camp

WILLIAMS FAMILY

Eliza Williams	F	25	
Baylis Williams	M	24	Died Dec. 16 in winter camp

WOLFINGER FAMILY

Mr. Wolfinger	M	?	Killed around Oct. 13, possibly by Reinhardt and Spitzer
Doris Wolfinger	F	?	

UNRELATED INDIVIDUALS

Mr. Hardkoop	M	60	Died around Oct. 8, abandoned by Lewis Keseberg
Patrick Dolan	M	40	Died Dec. 25 with snowshoers
Charles Stanton	M	35	Died around Dec. 21 with snowshoers
Charles Burger	M	30	Died Dec. 29 in winter camp
Joseph Reinhardt	M	30	Died in Nov. or early Dec. in winter camp
Augustus Spitzer	M	30	Died Feb. 7 in winter camp
John Denton	M	28	Died Feb. 24 with first rescue team
Milton Elliot	M	28	Died Feb. 9 in winter camp
Luke Halloran	M	25	Died Aug. 29 of consumption
William Herron	M	25	
Samuel Shoemaker	M	25	Died in Nov. or early Dec. in winter camp
James Smith	M	25	Died in Nov. or early Dec. in winter camp
John Snyder	M	25	Killed Oct. 5 by James Reed
Jean Trubode	M	23	
Antoine	M	23	Died Dec. 24 with snowshoers
Noah James	M	20	

Lists based on "Living Through the Donner Party," Discover Magazine, *March 1992, 104.*

CHRONOLOGY

1846

April 15 The Donners and Reeds, along with their hired help, leave their homes in Springfield, Illinois, bound for California.

May 11 The Springfield Party reaches Independence, Missouri.

May 19 Donners and Reeds attach themselves to the Russell wagon train.

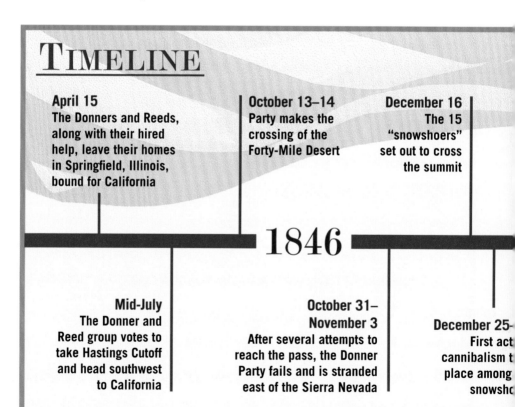

TIMELINE

April 15
The Donners and Reeds, along with their hired help, leave their homes in Springfield, Illinois, bound for California

October 13–14
Party makes the crossing of the Forty-Mile Desert

December 16
The 15 "snowshoers" set out to cross the summit

1846

Mid-July
The Donner and Reed group votes to take Hastings Cutoff and head southwest to California

October 31– November 3
After several attempts to reach the pass, the Donner Party fails and is stranded east of the Sierra Nevada

December 25–
First act cannibalism t place among snowsh

May 29   Elderly Sarah Keyes, Margaret Reed's mother, dies in Kansas Territory from a long-term illness.

June   The Russell caravan crosses Nebraska Territory, usually following the Platte River. Additional families attach themselves to the train.

Mid-July   While the main Russell Party continues on to Oregon, the Donner and Reed group votes to take Hastings Cutoff and head southwest to California. After George Donner is voted as the party's leader, the group becomes known as the Donner Party.

July 26 to 30   Donner Party reaches Fort Bridger in Wyoming, the last supply stop on the Hastings Cutoff before reaching the Sierra Nevada.

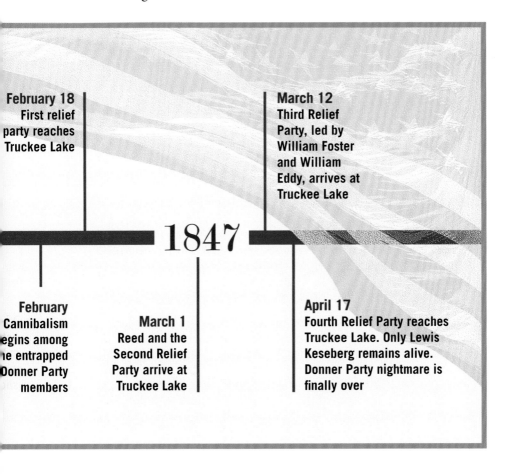

February 18
First relief party reaches Truckee Lake

March 12
Third Relief Party, led by William Foster and William Eddy, arrives at Truckee Lake

1847

February
Cannibalism begins among the entrapped Donner Party members

March 1
Reed and the Second Relief Party arrive at Truckee Lake

April 17
Fourth Relief Party reaches Truckee Lake. Only Lewis Keseberg remains alive. Donner Party nightmare is finally over

July 31	Party leaves Fort Bridger and follows Hastings Cutoff in modern-day Utah.
Early August	When Donner Party reaches Weber Canyon, the emigrants become stalled. Three members of the party ride ahead to contact Lansford Hastings, who is leading another wagon party along the trail.
August 25	Luke Halloran, who has been befriended by the Donners, dies of consumption on the trail.
Early September	Donner Party makes its nightmarish crossing of the Great Salt Lake Desert. When water runs short, the oxen collapse and run off when unhitched. The Reeds and others abandon some of their wagons.
September 10	With the party running low on food, Charles Stanton and William McCutchen ride ahead toward Sutter's Fort in California for fresh supplies.
October 5	After murdering John Snyder in self-defense, James Reed is banished from the Donner Party. Reed rides ahead to reach Sutter's Fort.
October 8 to 9	Mr. Hardkoop dies along the trail. Margaret Reed is forced to abandon her last wagon due to a shortage of oxen.
October 13 to 14	Party crosses the Forty-Mile Desert. During the crossing, Mr. Wolfinger is mysteriously murdered.
Mid-October	Donner Party reaches Truckee Meadows and rests before heading into the Sierra Nevada.
Late October	Charles Stanton returns to the Donner Party with fresh supplies, along with two Miwok men, Luis and Salvador. In the meantime, Reed arrives at Sutter's Fort, where he finds McCutchen, who has been held up by an illness. In the Sierra, the first major snowfall of the season begins with almost no let up until November 11.

October 27 to 30	Badly separated, the majority of the Donner party arrives at Truckee Lake (now called Donner Lake) on the Nevada-California border. Snows and accidents postpone the party's effort to cross the pass.
October 31 to November 3	After several attempts to reach the pass, the Donner Party fails and is stranded east of the Sierra Nevada. Meanwhile, Reed and McCutchen have been stopped from crossing the mountains from the opposite side, due to snowfall on October 31. They return to Sutter's Fort.
Late November	A party of 22 emigrants desperately tries to cross the pass, but fails. Death soon stalks the Donner Party.
November 25 to December 3	Second large snowstorm takes place at the pass.
December 9 to 13	Third heavy snowstorm piles the snow higher.
December 16	The 15 "snowshoers" set out to cross the summit.
December 25 to 27	First acts of cannibalism take place among the snowshoers.

1847

January 4 to 8	Desperate, Margaret and Virginia Reed, Milt Elliott, and Eliza Williams try to cross the summit but fail and return to camp.
January 10	Snowshoer William Foster kills the two Miwok men, Luis and Salvador, for food.
Mid-January	American Indians lead the remaining stranded and starving snowshoers out of the Sierra Nevada to safety. Half of the party is dead and most of them were cannibalized.
January 31	The First Relief Party, led by Aquilla Glover, leaves Sutter's Fort for the Sierra Nevada.

February	Cannibalism begins among the entrapped Donner Party members, although the Reeds appear to have abstained.
February 7	Second Relief Party, led by James Reed, leaves Yerba Buena.
February 18	First Relief Party reaches Truckee Lake.
February 22	First Relief Party leaves with 23 people rescued, including the Reed family. Soon, Patty and Tommy Reed have to turn back.
February 27	Margaret, Virginia, and Jimmy Reed are reunited with James Reed with the Second Relief Party.
March 1	Reed and the Second Relief Party arrive at Truckee Lake.
March 3	Second Relief Party leaves Truckee Lake with 17 people rescued.
March 6 to 8	Snowstorm strands Second Relief Party. Some members of the party decide to remain in the mountains to wait for the Third Relief Party.
March 12	Third Relief Party, led by William Foster and William Eddy, arrives at Truckee Lake.
March 13	Third Relief Party leaves with four rescued people.
April 17	Fourth Relief Party reaches Truckee Lake. Only Lewis Keseberg remains alive.
April 20	Fourth Relief Party leaves Truckee Lake with Keseberg. Donner Party nightmare is finally over.

NOTES

CHAPTER 1

1. Ralph Moody, *The Old Trails West: The Stories of the Trails That Made a Nation* (New York: Promontory Press, 1963), 274.
2. *Ibid.*, 280.
3. *Ibid.*
4. Marian Place, *Westward on the Oregon Trail* (New York: American Heritage Publishing, 1962), 104.

CHAPTER 2

1. Moody, 270.
2. Tom Bodett, *America's Historic Trails* (San Francisco: KQED Books, 1997), 175.
3. *Ibid.*
4. David Lavender, *The American Heritage History of The Great West* (New York: American Heritage Publishing, 1965), 101.
5. Bodett, 175.
6. Lavender, 101.
7. Bodett, 176.
8. Moody, 217.

CHAPTER 3

1. Bodett, 178.
2. *Ibid.*, 182.
3. *Ibid.*
4. Moody, 282.
5. Peter R. Limburg, *Deceived: The Story of the Donner Party* (Pacifica, CA: International Publishing Services, 1998), 11.
6. *Ibid.*
7. Moody, 282.
8. *Ibid.*

CHAPTER 4

1. George R. Stewart. *Ordeal by Hunger* (New York: Washington Square Press, 1960), 11.
2. *Ibid.*
3. *Ibid.*
4. *Ibid.*, 13.
5. *Ibid.*
6. *Ibid.*, 15.
7. Limburg, 14.
8. *Ibid.*, 16.
9. Marian Calabro, *The Perilous Journey of The Donner Party* (New York: Clarion Books, 1999), 21.
10. Limburg, 16.
11. Calabro, 22.
12. *Ibid.*
13. *Ibid.*, 26.
14. *Ibid.*, 32.

CHAPTER 5

1. Limburg, 27.
2. Calabro, 34.
3. Susan G. Butruille, *Women's Voices From the Oregon Trail: The Times That Tried Women's Souls* (Boise, ID: Tamarack Books, 1993), 155.
4. C.F. McGlashan, *History of the Donner Party: A Tragedy of the Sierra* (Stanford, CA: Stanford University Press, 1947), 26–27.
5. Limburg, 29.
6. *Ibid.*
7. Calabro, 36.
8. *Ibid.*, 37.
9. Limburg, 43.
10. *Ibid.*, 44.
11. Kenneth Holmes, ed., *Covered Wagon Women: Diaries & Letters from the*

Western Trails, 1840–1849, Volume I (Lincoln: University of Nebraska Press, 1983), 73.

12. Stewart, 15.
13. *Ibid.*
14. *Ibid.*
15. Calabro, 41.
16. *Ibid.*
17. *Ibid.*, 46.

CHAPTER 6

1. Limburg, 53.
2. *Ibid.*, 55.
3. Calabro, 50.
4. Limburg, 55.
5. Marc Simmons, et al., *Trails West* (Washington, DC: National Geographic Society, 1979), 128.
6. Calabro, 52.
7. *Ibid.*, 56.
8. Limburg, 66.
9. Calabro, 57.
10. Limburg, 59.
11. Calabro, 59.
12. *Ibid.*, 60.
13. Limburg, 69.
14. Calabro, 61.
15. *Ibid.*, 63.

CHAPTER 7

1. Calabro, 63.
2. Limburg, 80.
3. Calabro, 70.
4. *Ibid.*, 71.
5. Limburg, 102.
6. *Ibid.*, 104.
7. Calabro, 85.
8. *Ibid.*

CHAPTER 8

1. Calabro, 86–87.
2. *Ibid.*, 87.
3. Limburg, 113.
4. Calabro, 91.

5. Frank Mullen, Jr., *The Donner Party Chronicles: A Day-by-Day Account of a Doomed Wagon Train, 1846–1847* (Reno: A Halcyon Imprint of the Nevada Humanities Committee, 1997), 228.
6. Calabro, 92.
7. *Ibid.*, 97.
8. *Ibid.*, 98.
9. *Ibid.*
10. *Ibid.*
11. *Ibid.*, 100.
12. *Ibid.*, 101.
13. *Ibid.*, 102.
14. *Ibid.*
15. *Ibid.*, 104.
16. *Ibid.*, 107.
17. *Ibid.*
18. Limburg, 130.
19. *Ibid.*, 165.

CHAPTER 9

1. Calabro, 113.
2. Limburg, 165.
3. Calabro, 113.
4. Limburg, 168.
5. *Calabro*, 117.
6. *Ibid.*, 118.
7. *Ibid.*, 119.
8. *Ibid.*
9. *Ibid.*, 120.
10. Limburg, 175.
11. *Ibid.*, 176.
12. *Ibid.*, 177.
13. *Ibid.*
14. *Ibid.*, 179.
15. *Ibid.*
16. *Ibid.*, 180.
17. *Ibid.*, 187.

CHAPTER 10

1. *Ibid.*
2. *Ibid.*, 198.

3. *Ibid.*

4. *Ibid.*

5. *Ibid.*, 200.

6. *Ibid.*

7. *Ibid.*

8. *Ibid.*, 201.

9. *Ibid.*, 207.

10. Jared Diamond, "Living Through the Donner Party,"

Discover Magazine, March 1992, 105.

11. Limburg, 211.

12. *Ibid.*

CHAPTER 11

1. Calabro, 152.

BIBLIOGRAPHY

Bodett, Tom. *America's Historic Trails.* San Francisco: KQED Books, 1997.

Butruille, Susan G. *Women's Voices From the Oregon Trail: The Times That Tried Women's Souls.* Boise, Id.: Tamarack Books, 1993.

Calabro, Marian. *The Perilous Journey of the Donner Party.* New York: Clarion Books, 1999.

Diamond, Jared. "Living Through the Donner Party." *Discover Magazine,* March 1992.

Goldfield, Allen. *The American Journey: A History of the United States.* Upper Saddle River, N.J.: Pearson-Prentice Hall, 2004.

Hawgood, John A. *America's Western Frontiers: The Exploration and Settlement of the Trans-Mississippi West.* New York: Alfred A. Knopf, 1967.

Holmes, Kenneth L., ed. *Covered Wagon Women: Diaries & Letters from the Western Trails, 1840–1849.* Volume I. Lincoln: University of Nebraska Press, 1983.

Horn, Huston. *The Pioneers.* New York: Time-Life Books, 1974.

Houghton, Eliza P. Donner. *The Expedition of the Donner Party and Its Tragic Fate.* Lincoln: University of Nebraska Press, 1997.

Lavender, David. *The American Heritage History of the Great West.* New York: American Heritage Publishing, 1965.

———. *Snowbound: The Tragic Story of the Donner Party.* New York: Holiday House, 1996.

Limburg, Peter R. *Deceived: The Story of the Donner Party.* Pacifica, Ca.: International Publishing Services, 1998.

McGlashan, C.F. *History of the Donner Party: A Tragedy of the Sierra.* Stanford, Cal.: Stanford University Press, 1947.

McNeese, Tim. *The American Frontier.* St. Louis, Mo.: Milliken Publishing Company, 2002.

————. *History in the Making: Sources and Essays of America's Past.* Volume I. New York: American Heritage, 1994.

Moody, Ralph. *The Old Trails West: The Stories of the Trails That Made a Nation.* New York: Promontory Press, 1963.

Mullen, Frank Jr. *The Donner Party Chronicles: A Day-by-Day Account of a Doomed Wagon Train, 1846–1847.* Reno: A Halcyon Imprint of the Nevada Humanities Committee, 1997.

Place, Marian T. *Westward on the Oregon Trail.* New York: American Heritage Publishing, 1962.

Simmons, Marc, et al. *Trails West.* Washington, D.C.: National Geographic Society, 1979.

Stewart, George. *Ordeal by Hunger.* New York: Washington Square Press, 1960.

Unruh, John D. Jr. *The Plains Across: The Overland Emigrants and Trans-Mississippi West, 1840–1860.* Urbana: University of Illinois Press, 1982.

Further Reading

Houston, James D. *Snow Mountain Passage*. New York: Harcourt, 2002.

Murphy, Virginia Reed. *Across the Plains in the Donner Party*. Nottingham, England: Shoe String Press, 1996.

Pelta, Kathy. *Trails to the West: Beyond the Mississippi*. Austin, Tex.: Raintree Steck-Vaughn, 1998.

Wachtel, Roger. *Donner Party*. New York: Children's Press, 2003.

Welveart, Scott R. *Donner Party*. Mankato, Minn.: Coughlan Publishing, 2006.

Werther, Scott P. *Donner Party*. New York: Scholastic Library Publishing, 2002.

WEB SITES

American Experience: The Donner Party
http://www.pbs.org/wgbh/amex/donner

The Donner Party
http://www.micmacmedia.com/Donner_Party/donner_party.html

New Light on the Donner Party
http://www.utahcrossroads.org/DonnerParty

The Virtual Museum of the City of San Francisco
http://www.sfmuseum.org/hist6/donner.html

Photo Credits

Index

Alder Creek, 81–83, 99, 103
American Indians, 70, 73, 77,
    86–87, 89–91, 115. *See also*
    specific tribes

Bartelson, John, 13. *See also*
    Bidwell-Bartelson Party
Bear Flag Revolt, 65
Bidwell, John, 12, 18, 19
Bidwell-Bartelson Party, 12–19,
    23
Black Hawk War, 34, 49
Boggs, Lillburn, 41
Bonney, Wales, 52
Breen, John, 63, 85–86, 96,
    111–112
Breen, Mary, 106–107
Breen, Patrick
    cannibalism and, 98–99,
        110–111
    departure of, 76
    on American Indians, 86–87
    overview of, 50–51
    Third Relief Party and, 106
    water and, 73–74
Bridger, Fort, 52, 57–59
Bridger, Jim, 13, 58
"Broken Hand" (Thomas Fitz-
    patrick), 13–15, 24
Buchanan, James, 65
Burger, "Dutch Charley," 51

Cady, Charles, 103, 105, 107–108
California Trail, 16, 19, 21, 23,
    64–65
cannibalism, 87–92, 98–99,
    102, 104–105, 111–112, 115,
    118–119

Cheyenne Tribe, 15
Chimney Rock, 47
Clark, Nicholas, 103–104, 105,
    113
Clay, Henry, 41
Clyman, James, 47–49, 52
consumption, 45, 61–63
Continental Divide, 52
Courthouse Rock, 47
cutoffs, 27, 55, 58. *See also* Hast-
    ings Cutoff

De Smet, Pierre Jean, 13, 15
Denton, John, 36, 96, 110
Digger Tribes, 70, 115
Dolan, Patrick, 51, 82, 83, 89
Donner, Elizabeth, 35, 96, 105
Donner, George
    cannibalism of, 115
    injury, illness and, 77, 83, 96,
        102–104, 112–113
    as leader, 56, 72
    McCutchen and, 59
    overview of, 30, 32–33, 36
    wagons and, 68
Donner, Isaac, 106, 111
Donner, Jacob, 35, 66–67, 83, 96,
    99, 104–105
Donner, Mary, 106, 111
Donner, Tamsen
    cannibalism of, 119
    concerns of, 55
    good health of, 96, 102
    Halloran and, 61–62
    history of, 30
    Independence and, 40–41
    loss of wagons and, 68
    Nebraska and, 46–47

overview of, 33, 36
on people of company, 51
refusal of to leave husband,
105, 112–114
swindling of, 103–104
Donner Lake. *See* Truckee Lake
Dry Sandy Creek, 53

Eddy, James, 50, 85, 102, 105,
108–110
Eddy, William
fate of, 121–122
"Forlorn Hope" group and,
83, 90–92
hunting by, 82
lack of cannibalism by, 88–90
loss of wagon and, 73–75
overview of, 50
Third Rescue Party and,
108–110, 112
Elliott, Milt, 36, 70, 84, 86, 99,
102
*Emigrants' Guide to Oregon and
California, The* (Hastings), 23,
26, 37

First Rescue Party, 93–98, 100
Fitzpatrick, Thomas, 13–15, 24
"Forlorn Hope" group, 83
Forty-Mile Desert, 4, 55, 73
Foster, Georgie, 102, 104, 105
Foster, Joseph, 5, 8
Foster, William
cannibalism and murder by,
89–90, 121
death of Pike and, 76
overview of, 50
survival of, 92
Third Rescue Party and, 108,
112–113, 115
Fourth Relief Party, 113–119
Frémont, John C., 27, 31, 64–65,
90

graves, defiling of, 54
Graves, Franklin, 60, 83, 89, 111
Graves, Franklin, Jr., 106
Graves, Mary Ann, 83, 89, 111,
122
Great Britain, 20, 31
Green River, 57
Greenwood, Caleb, 3, 55
Greenwood Cutoff, 55, 58
Guadelupe-Hidalgo, Treaty of,
65

Hall, Fort, 55, 56
Halloran, Luke, 51, 61–63
Hardkoop family, 51, 72–73
Hastings, Lansford W.
directions of, 52, 57–60, 63
guidebook of, 23, 24–26, 31, 37
Hastings Cutoff, 3, 27, 47–49,
52–55, 69
Herron, Walter, 36, 72, 75
Humboldt River, 15, 18, 69, 73
Humboldt Sink, 3–4

illness, 45, 61–63, 72–73
Independence Rock, 24, 49, 52

James, Noah, 36, 116
Johnson's Ranch, 100, 108, 122

Kansa Tribe, 43
Kearney, Fort, 47
Kelley, Hall Jackson, 20–21
Keseberg, Lewis
cannibalism by, 104, 112, 114,
118–119
conflicts with, 51, 54
fate of, 122–123
grave robbery by, 54
injury to, 97
Second Rescue Party and, 102
Keseberg family, 96, 98, 99
Keyes, Sarah, 34, 45–46, 116

Lakota Tribe, 24, 49, 54
Laramie, Fort, 47
Little Sandy River, 53–55, 57
Louisiana Territory, 28–29

Manifest Destiny, 28–29
Masons, 30, 34, 63, 98
McClellan, George B., 75
McCutchen, Harriet, 85
McCutchen, William, 59, 70, 83,
    100, 101–102
Mexican-American War, 42–43,
    64, 90–91
Miller, Hiram, 56, 59, 107, 110
Miwok guides, 75, 78, 83, 89–90,
    117
Montgomery, Allen, 5, 8
murders
    cannibalism and, 89–90, 104,
        112, 117
    Keseberg and, 122–123
    of Snyder, 70–72
    of Wolfinger, 73
Murphy, John, 96, 124
Murphy, John Landrum, 85
Murphy, Lavina, 50, 98–99,
    101–102, 105, 112, 113
Murphy, Lem, 89
Murphy, Mary, 122
Murphy, Simon, 105, 113

Nueva Helvetia, 17

Oregon Country, 10, 20

Paiute Tribe, 3–4
Palo Alto, Battle of, 43
Pico, Pio, 17, 23
Pike, Catherine, 96
Pike, Naomi, 96, 98
Pike, William, 50, 75–76
Pioneer Palace Car, 39
Platte River, 54
Polk, James K., 42–43, 65, 90–91

Reed, James
    fate of, 123–124
    Hastings Cutoff and, 58,
        60–61
    overview of, 30, 34
    oxen of, 53–54
    rescue party of, 75, 83, 93,
        101–102, 107
    suffering of, 68–72
    Wyoming and, 47–51
Reed, Margaret
    death of mother of, 45
    escape party of, 84–85
    fate of, 123–124
    First Rescue Party and, 98–99
    injury to, 70
    meat and, 82
    Reed wagon and, 39
Reed, Patty, 86, 98, 100, 105,
    107, 124
Reed, Tommy, 98, 99, 100, 105,
    107
Reed, Virginia
    on bargaining by mother, 82
    concern for Tommy Reed
        and, 99
    death of grandmother and,
        45–46
    effects of snowfall and, 78
    fate of, 124
    on hunger and suffering,
        84–86
    Independence Rock and,
        49–50
    loss of oxen and, 66–67
    pony and, 34
    on wagon, 37, 39
Reinhardt, Joseph, 51, 73
Ruby Mountains, 69
Russell, William H., 41, 55

Sacramento Valley, 17
Santa Anna (General), 91
Santa Fe Trail, 12

Sapling Grove, 12–13
Schallenberger, Moses, 2, 4, 7–9
Scott's Bluff, 47
Second Rescue Party, 99–104,
   110
Shoemaker, Samuel, 36, 99
Slidell, John, 43
Snyder, John, 70–72
South Pass, 52–53
Spitzer, Augustus, 51, 73, 85
Springfield, Illinois, 27–31
Stanton, Charles T., 51, 70, 75,
   78, 83, 87–88
Starks, John, 110, 111, 113
statistics on disaster, 116–118
Stevens Party, 2–9, 21, 77
Stone, Charles, 103–104, 105,
   107–108, 110
survivors, 120–129
Sutter, John, 4, 16–18, 19
Sutter's Fort, 4–5, 7, 17–18, 24,
   29, 75
Sweetwater River, 52

Taylor, Zachary, 43, 90–91
Third Relief Party, 103, 108–113
Thornton, Jessy Quinn, 41, 55
Townshend, John, 2, 5
Trubode, Jean-Baptiste, 59, 96,
   104, 105, 113, 116

Truckee Lake, 77, 80
Truckee River, 4–5, 74–75
tuberculosis (consumption), 45,
   61–63
Tucker, Reason, 95, 113

Vallejo, Mariano, 65
Vasquez, Louis, 58
violence. *See* sighting; murders
voting for route selection, 56

Wakaruska Creek, 41
Walker, Joe, 21
Ward, Franklin Jr., 111
Wasatch Range, 59
water supplies, 63–64, 66, 74
Weber River, 59, 60
Western Emigration Society,
   12–19
White, Elijah, 23–24
Williams, Baylis, 36, 83
Williams, Eliza, 84, 96
Winnemuca, Sarah, 87
Wolfinger family, 51, 73
Woodworth, Selim E., 108–110,
   115
Wyoming, 47–50, 59

ABOUT THE AUTHOR

TIM McNEESE lives on a cutoff route of the Oregon Trail, where he is associate professor of history at York College in York, Nebraska. He is in his seventeenth year of college instruction. McNeese earned an associate of arts degree from York College, a bachelor of arts in history and political science from Harding University, and a master of arts in history from Missouri State University. A prolific author of books for elementary, middle and high school, and college readers, McNeese has published more than 90 books and educational materials over the past 20 years, on everything from the civil rights movement to Spanish painters. His writing has earned him a citation in the library reference work *Contemporary Authors* and multiple citations in *Best Books for Young Teen Readers*. In 2006, McNeese appeared on the History Channel program "Risk Takers/History Makers: John Wesley Powell and the Grand Canyon." He was a faculty member at the 2006 Tony Hillerman Writers Conference in Albuquerque, where he lectured on the American Indians of the Southwest. McNeese and his wife, Beverly, sponsored study trips for college students on the Lewis and Clark Trail in 2003 and 2005 and to the American Southwest in 2008. Feel free to contact Professor McNeese at tdmcneese@york.edu.